W9-CRE-402

Breaking
Through
to Each Other

Breaking Through to Each Other

Creative Persuasion on the
Job and in the Home

Jesse S. Nirenberg, Ph.D.

Harper & Row, Publishers
New York, Hagerstown
San Francisco, London

BREAKING THROUGH TO EACH OTHER: CREATIVE PERSUASION ON THE JOB
AND IN THE HOME. Copyright © 1976 by Jesse S. Nirenberg, Ph.D. All
rights reserved. Printed in the United States of America. No part of this
book may be used or reproduced in any manner whatsoever without written permission except in the case of brief quotations embodied in critical
articles and reviews. For information address Harper & Row, Publishers,
Inc., 10 East 53rd Street, New York, N.Y. 10022. Published simulta-
neously in Canada by Fitzhenry & Whiteside Limited, Toronto.
FIRST EDITION

Library of Congress Cataloging in Publication Data

Nirenberg, Jesse S
    Breaking through to each other.
    Includes index.
    1. Persuasion (Psychology)   2.   Psychology, Industrial.   I.   Title.
BF637.P4N57   1976   158'.2   74–1841
ISBN 0–06–013207–8

---

76 77 78 79 10 9 8 7 6 5 4 3 2 1

To my wife Edna,

and my daughters, Liz, Sheila, Nina

And to my parents, May and Abraham,

and my sister, Cleo

Contents

1 How We Lose Each Other in Conversation

Imagine yourself communicating with another person, mind to mind. No words are uttered. Each of you induces your own mental image and emotions in the mind of the other. Now compare that direct hook-up with verbal communication, and you can appreciate the hurdles imposed by words. Pictures impart a mass of information instantly, but words are sent and received one at a time, conveying information over a time span.

Jumping to Conclusions

Communicating over a time span makes misinterpretation more likely, for minds are in continuous motion. The receiver is a moving target, mentally springing back and forth between his own thoughts and the sender's ongoing message. As information comes to us, we quickly form conclusions, revising them to fit additional information as it arrives. We don't wait until all the information is in to form a picture; our mind jumps ahead, filling in the missing parts in order to form the whole.

Most people, for example, will see a face in Figure A rather than just three horizontal lines and one vertical line. They mentally fill in the missing features. In Figure B they see a triangle instead of just three circles, again mentally filling in connecting lines that are not there.

As we lead up to our point, our listener may jump to the wrong conclusion about what we're getting at. And if he doesn't

FIGURE A.   FIGURE B.

like what he thinks we're getting at, he may become defensive or
tune out and leave with a misunderstanding.

Listen to a subordinate form a succession of wrong conclusions as his boss leads up to the point:

Boss:	As a supervisor, one of your most important func- tions is to bring others along, to help them become more productive.
Subordinate:	(*To himself:* I wonder why he's telling me that.)
Boss:	A lot of supervisors don't realize this and instead of working with their subordinates to show them how to improve, they spend most of their time planning and assigning work and criticizing with- out being constructive about it.
Subordinate:	(*To himself:* He's going to tell me I don't work with my people enough. Well, he's all wrong. I'm responsive as hell. I really listen.)
Boss:	Still, some of these supervisors have the capability. They could be developed but they need training. I noted that the University has an evening course in human relations for supervisors.
Subordinate:	(*To himself:* He wants me to take a course. I'm the last guy that needs a course in human rela- tions.)
Boss:	You get along very well with your people and I'd like your opinion on whether it would be worth- while to send some of our supervisors to this course—those who are having difficulty getting along with others.
Subordinate:	(*To himself:* Why didn't he say so in the first place?)

Sometimes a trace of paranoia emerges and we jump to the
conclusion that the other person is rejecting us, treating us un-

fairly, or being inconsiderate. We overlook those interpretations that do not involve us personally. On the phone, for example, if the other person responds meagerly, we may feel that he doesn't want to talk to us, when actually he may have a visitor or another call waiting. A child may want to know why he is being picked on when asked to do a chore. And when the price seems too low, we wonder what's wrong with the merchandise.

We increase the chances that the other person will jump to wrong conclusions when we creep up on our point by way of a lot of preliminary reasoning, trying to get everything in before we get to that point. Perhaps we're afraid our idea will be rejected or misinterpreted, thereby ending the discussion. Actually, it could be just the beginning. The reply to *no* can very well be *why not?* And a misinterpretation is much less likely if the other person knows from the start where we're going.

Making Assumptions About the Other Person's Premises

When the other person raises an objection to our proposal, we often answer his objection by making an assumption about his underlying thinking.

For example, if we propose a procedure, and the other fellow says that it's too complicated, we come right back with an explanation of how simple it is, assuming that by *complicated* he means it will be too difficult. But maybe the other fellow isn't concerned with difficulty, but with how long it will take. And if he does object that it will take too long, we may respond by making an assumption about what he means by *too long*.

A mother tells her teenage daughter, "I want you to come right home after school instead of hanging around with your friends." The daughter jumps to the conclusion that her mother doesn't like the daughter's friends. However, the mother may be expecting a package to be delivered that afternoon, intends to be out, and wants her daughter to be home to receive it.

A doctor tells a patient to take his medicine before each meal. The patient assumes that the medicine helps his digestion.

Actually, the doctor only wants to associate the medicine with three scheduled events during the day so that the patient will establish a regular habit of taking his medicine.

A prospect tells a salesman, "I don't think your machine will work as well for us as the one we're using." The salesman replies, "Our machine will be perfect for you. It can turn out twenty per cent more work, and it has more adjustments and controls on it so that you can adapt it to a greater variety of work." The prospect responds, "That's just it. Your machine is too complicated. It will only confuse our people and we'd have to invest more time in training them. It's not for us."

When the other person tells us that we have presented him with a particularly difficult problem, how can we know without further inquiry whether he means that it will take a lot of effort, that the chances of solving it are slim, or that he wants a lot of credit if he does solve it?

Tuning Out

While every person is aware that he tunes in and out of conversations, he always seems to think that the other person listens steadily to him. This illusion is encouraged by the listener's periodically nodding or saying "uh huh."

See the effect of tuning out in a business discussion:

Sales Manager: I think we ought to get the salesmen together at meetings, by regions, starting the last week in November. We could then introduce the new product, tell them about the change in the bonus plan, and present the advertising plans for next year. And they could bring up any problems they have.

Vice President: Sounds good. I think we ought to do it by regions instead of bringing the whole sales force together. When did you have in mind? The middle of December would be good. The salesmen aren't so busy. We could get out for two days to each of the four regions, running two meetings in each week.

(The Vice President evidently missed the Sales Manager's suggestion of the last week in November; and it sounds as though he missed the Sales Manager's suggestion that they run the meetings by regions since the Vice President also suggested it.)

Sales Manager: If we run two meetings in one week, we'll have to keep the men on Saturday. I don't think we'll be as productive that way. Maybe we could cut the meetings to two days if we worked evenings.

(The Sales Manager must have tuned out when the Vice President mentioned two days. The Sales Manager was probably thinking of his own idea of three days and somehow assumed that the Vice President was also thinking of three days.)

Emotional Distraction

Much conversation is motivated by emotions, by the need to put a feeling into words in order to communicate it to someone. To discharge anger, one needs a target and an angry thought to wrap the words around. Anxiety moves us to talk, to master our worries by putting them into words, and to seek reassurance from others. Guilt causes us to talk apologetically and to confess what we blame ourselves for. And joy we yearn to share.

Listen to the play of feeling take over in a husband-wife conversation:

Wife: You know, John, I was speaking to Millie, and she said that in Tokyo the people are so pleasant and polite. And yet they'll bump into you and push you around in the subway like it's natural.

(The wife is leading up to a suggestion that she and her husband take a trip, and she is trying to "prepare" him.)

Husband: Am I glad I don't have to take the subway anymore. It's a killer.

(The husband, from past conversations, probably knows where his wife is heading. He resents her indirection and is irritated by her attempt to manipulate him. To get even he tries to sidetrack the conversation.)

Wife: She said the food was delicious. She thinks they cook better than we do, in the restaurants, I mean.

(The wife ignores her husband's attempt to sidetrack. She probably senses the hostility implicit in his ignoring her opening and tries to eliminate that hostility in a way that can only increase it—persisting in pursuing her own line of thinking while evading his.)

Husband: Yeah, I like Chinese food.

(He carries on his attack with another sidetrack and a deliberate misinterpretation.)

Wife: Not Chinese, Japanese. And the people are so friendly and polite, and the service is so good. She enjoyed it more than the time she went to Europe.

(She pauses only to correct him and then doggedly pursues her own path, unrealistically hoping he'll follow, even though he's obviously moving in a different direction.)

Husband: Millie is always dragging her husband around, all over the world. I bet Hal would give anything to be able to relax in a cottage with clear mountain air and cool streams and all those trout just asking for the bait. And speaking of food, I'd trade all that chop suey for a helping of the pan fried fish we catch.

(He doesn't want to play the game of indirection any longer; he indicates openly that he is opposed to traveling abroad when he guesses that Hal doesn't like it.)

Wife: They don't eat chop suey, Frank. They're Japanese. That's the trouble, Frank, you don't know anything outside of your little world.

(Now that the game is over, her anger surfaces and she launches a frontal attack, striking at his self-image.)

Husband: Okay, so maybe I don't know what the Japanese eat. Maybe they eat bugs or worms or grass. But there aren't any coming for dinner, anyway, so who cares?

(He goes on the defensive.)

Wife: It's a good thing they're not, because you wouldn't know how to act.

(She mounts a still sharper attack.)

Husband: Is that so? Well, all you've got to do is be yourself. That's the way to act with everyone. They respect you for it.

(He defends again.)

Wife: Not you, Frank. They only respect you when you keep your mouth shut. Once you start talking, you might as well give up. Listen, Frank, for once in our lives let's get out and see what's going on. Let's go anywhere— London, Paris, maybe even Spain.

(All her fury emerges, and then, too late, she returns to her plea.)

Husband: Forget it. I don't need any trips just to impress people. Either they take me as I am, or to hell with them. Now, if you haven't anything better to talk about, shut up and let me read the paper.

(Now he strikes back.)

A person is most vulnerable to verbal hurt in his sense of self-worth. When we characterize someone as undesirable in some respect—as selfish, stupid, or greedy—we hurt him because we're generalizing about him. This is quite different from telling someone he did something undesirable in a particular situation. A person can act selfishly or stupidly on one occasion and still feel that he is basically kind or bright. He might even regard the criticism of a particular act as useful information.

Overloading Remarks

When we extend a remark too much, we often lose the other person, who can only hold on to so much information at a time. When we give him too much information he starts losing some of it, like a shopper trying to carry more packages than his arms and fingers can grasp: As he bends down to pick up one, he loses another.

An overloaded remark also frustrates another person. As we talk, the other person hears information to which he wants to respond. But since we go on talking, he has to suppress his desire to add or to disagree—or else he has to interrupt. If he doesn't interrupt, he's distracted by his wanting to; if he does, the conversation may be sidetracked. If we make too many overloaded remarks, the other person's need to talk will be denied satisfaction, and he will withdraw mentally, even while looking attentive.

Personal Premises That Prevent Realistic Thinking

One of the most powerful blocks to communicating is the tendency to interpret reality so that it fits a set of personal views. We tend to hold these personal views as unshakable truths, and they become solid premises in our reasoning.

A salesman, for example, may hold the view that the more he talks in the sales interview, the more effective he is. As a result, he dominates each conversation, giving prospects little opportunity to express their own concerns. When the salesman loses sales he blames the product, the competition, or the prospect. He may even blame himself for not talking enough. And when the manager tells the salesman he talks too much, he concludes that the manager must have observed or reasoned wrongly.

As another example, let's say that a person carries deep within him the view that when he takes a risk, the chances are always much greater that he will lose than that he will win. He is therefore reluctant to take any risks, and he avoids making any changes, because to change is to risk. He turns away new business procedures that could save him money, clings to old equipment, and rejects new ventures even when the odds are in his favor. When reaching for the truth, some of us question everything except these firmly planted premises. And thus the solution to the problem eludes us.

These anchored false premises, so familiar a part of our mental landscape, often make it difficult for us to get through to each other. While we try to explain to the other fellow why his conclusions are wrong and ours are right, he thinks only of his own reasoning, and how much more right it is than ours. We, in turn, do the same to him.

Look how his personal premises influence the boss's thinking in a conversation with a supervisor:

Supervisor: The cleaning machine broke down again. I think we ought to buy a new one. We're wasting a lot of time and money repairing it.

Boss: I know it's a nuisance, but I don't want to spend the money now. (*To himself:* When someone wants you to spend money it's safest to start by saying "no.")

Supervisor: I hate to keep talking about it, and I know a new machine is expensive, but I've made some estimates, and the way we're spending money on repairs I figure that we'll get back the cost of the new machine in two years on savings from repairs we won't have to make.

Boss: Two years. That sounds pretty good. Let's buy the less expensive machine and get our money back even sooner. (*To himself:* When someone wants to spend my money, if I don't make him justify it, he'll spend it carelessly.)

Supervisor: I don't think that would be wise. The less expensive machine will only cost us more in the long run. It won't last as long; it will need more maintenance; and it's not as versatile.

Boss: That's what the salesman says. But with a lot of

these high-priced machines you're just paying for the name. I think I'll stick with our machine a while longer and see how it goes. (*To himself:* When someone tries hard to get you to do something, there must be something in it for him personally.)

Resistance to Change

To varying degrees, everyone resists change. Changing involves the risk of losing time, effort, and money. When change offers reward we can't ignore it, though often we'd like to.

In the struggle to avoid change and the anxiety that goes with it, we might rationalize a higher cost and a lower gain than is realistic. We might exaggerate the trouble involved and project our own annoyance on others, deciding that they won't like it. And we might reason that if we're successful with what we're doing, there is no need for change—ignoring the possibility of being still more successful.

Rationalizing to resist change is a major block to communication. When we rationalize we avoid communicating, because the more we communicate, the more likely we are to encounter the truth.

See how one person, receiving a suggestion for change, immediately avoids considering it without asking for more information or encouraging further discussion:

Comptroller:	I think we ought to raise the limit on the value of purchases that department heads can make on their own. I've figured out, after surveying purchases over the last six months, that if we raise this limit from one hundred to three hundred dollars, we'll save about five thousand dollars a year in management time now wasted in discussing such purchases in order to get approval.
Vice President:	If we raise the limit on what they can buy without getting approval, a lot of money will be wasted on purchases that should never have been made.

The Vice President resisted the idea without even asking the comptroller how he arrived at a five-thousand-dollar-a-year saving.

Resistance to change is a familiar ingredient in family situations:

Father:	What do you say we go to a hockey game this weekend, for a change, instead of football?
Son:	I don't like hockey.
Father:	Did you ever see a hockey game?
Son:	No. I just know I won't like it, at least not as much as football.

Credibility Loss

People lose their credibility easily when they evade a question, reason wrongly, leave gaps in a story, or fill in gaps with guesses and assumptions. The result is often a disturbing mixture of hard fact and misinformation. Whether an individual deliberately deceives or is careless in transmitting information, other people are thereafter less receptive to his information. And once a person loses his credibility, it becomes much more difficult for him to communicate.

As a result of experience, for example, I have become quite skeptical about directions that strangers give me in the street. They want to be helpful and feel they can be even if they have only a slight notion of the directions I need. So they build on meager information with guesses and assumptions, and I wind up in the wrong place.

Mental Inertia

Being engaged in a conversation doesn't necessarily mean that we're thinking about what the other person is saying, nor even about what we're saying. In order to think we have to overcome mental inertia—a tendency to be mentally passive, our attention drifting to whatever enters our mind. Thinking purposefully—interpreting, comparing, classifying, deciding—requires self-discipline and effort.

Surface thinking dominates the following conversation between a teacher and a parent. Notice the lack of probing, of getting to specifics, of discovering causes and solutions:

Parent: Jimmy doesn't do too well in math. I was looking at his report card and math seems to be his worst subject. Funny, I was always good in math.

Teacher: Well, he doesn't seem to put much into his homework. He has only a vague idea of the math concepts.

Parent: I can't seem to get him away from the TV set. Between that and football he doesn't put much into his homework. They've always got something special coming up they have to do, whether it's a TV program or a game or something they have to buy.

Teacher: Well, you can't learn anything unless you work at it. He could have the best teacher in the world, but if he doesn't work, he won't learn.

Parent: When I was a kid there was no fooling around. We did our homework. My father was very strict. He asked all of us every night if we did our homework, and if we didn't, we were punished.

Teacher: Parents aren't what they used to be. They're too permissive. They spoil the children.

Parent: Listen, I'll have to get after Jimmy. He's a good kid but he gets restless. I always say to him, "Jimmy, if you don't learn now, when will you learn?" They have to build a firm foundation. I have to run now but I'm glad Jimmy has such a good teacher.

Ambiguity

Ironically, the very clarity of our own views frequently causes us to be ambiguous, to make remarks that can be interpreted in different ways. We see something so clearly that we're careless in describing it, unaware of other interpretations of our words.

Listen to a student describe his teacher to a friend:

"Boy, my science teacher is tough."

"You mean he's a hard marker."

"No, he's not such a hard marker. In fact, he's kind of generous. I got a B on the last test when I really should have gotten a C."

"Oh, he gives a lot of homework."

"No, not so much. Not like some of my other teachers."

"So, what do you mean he's tough?"

"I mean he expects you to really know the assignment. Not just read it. Know it. And he grills you the next day with all kinds of questions."

"So what's so tough about that? My history teacher gives us big assignments, grills us with questions, and marks hard, too. That's tough."

Ambiguity creeps in as soon as we relax our vigilance over the precision of our remarks and leave out that one essential bit of information. Ambiguity is carried in with every adjective; for what exactly do we mean by good or strong or expensive or durable or efficient—and how good or strong or expensive or durable or efficient is it? When is soon? When we say someone is smart, do we mean he has a lot of knowledge, he thinks quickly, he looks ahead, or he is interested in abstract ideas?

Look at all the ambiguities in this business conversation:

Sales Manager:	You've got to do something about getting shipments out on time. Customers are screaming about late deliveries.
	(How many customers? How late are deliveries?)
Production Manager:	Listen, Joe, we do the best we can. Your salesmen are making all kinds of promises about delivering sooner than we can even make the stuff. You've got to give us more time.
	(How many salesmen made how many promises? How unrealistic were these promises? How much time is wanted?)

Sales Manager:	The competition is fierce. They're making promises of quick delivery and they're keeping their promises. If they can do it, we ought to be able to.
	(*Which competing companies? What speed of delivery are they promising? How often are they keeping their promises?*)
Production Manager:	Look, you come down to the plant, and if you can show me how to make it faster, I'll listen. But until then, you better keep your salesmen honest.

They didn't get very far; how could they with all that ambiguity fogging up communication?

Since we do tune out, jump to conclusions, make assumptions, operate from false personal premises, are distracted by emotions, overload our remarks with information, resist change, listen passively without thinking, suffer credibility loss, and talk ambiguously, we have to learn how to talk to each other in a way that gets our message past these natural obstacles.

2 Empathizing

The most generous, compassionate people can often be quite selfish in conversation. They will interrupt constantly, finish other people's sentences for them, keep the other person waiting impatiently while they meander to the point, and explain to a fuming friend why he shouldn't be angry when the friend just can't wait to explode.

A conversation is often an ongoing conflict of interest. Frequently we can hardly contain ourselves until the other person finishes so that we can speak. And when another person tells us his thinking, working out his ideas aloud, how often do we leap in to challenge him on some point, interrupting his building of ideas and shattering his thought structure, rather than wait until he has finished? And how often do we make the other person a sounding board, only to get irritated when he doesn't see things our way?

We are also faced constantly with the pressure of our own needs in conversation—and it's much harder to be kind under pressure. When internal pressures mount, one turns inward and ignores the needs of others. And if we are not even aware of the needs of others in conversation, we can be drawn inward by very slight inner pressures.

Growing up, we learn to suppress our own needs at times for the sake of satisfying others'. We learn to share, to do favors, to say thank you, to wait in line. But we are rarely taught how to be helpful, patient, and considerate in conversation; we don't learn to feel for the other person when he is talking.

We are brought up to view talking primarily as idea interchange; we are only dimly conscious of its use for the sheer sake of self-expression, for working out one's ideas and feelings, discharging super-heated emotion, expressing love, and sharing the human experience. What we need, beginning in childhood, is a continuous consciousness raising in verbal interaction.

Raising our consciousness of conversational needs can begin by looking at our own wants. How do we expect our conversational partner to behave? When you're talking and the other person is unresponsive, do you become anxious that he's not listening? Would you feel more comfortable if he gave some definite sign that he's paying attention?

When we ask a question that is answered with another question, aren't we irritated at the refusal to give us the information we want? and at the expectation, at the same time, that we will respond to the new question? While answering question with question might seem clever if one viewed the conversation as a duel, isn't it self-defeating? And when someone asks us question after question, without telling us why he's asking each question and what he's making of the answers we give him, don't we feel pushed around?

Once we become aware of what gives us pleasure and what frustrates us in conversational behavior, we can empathize by imagining how we would feel if the other person behaved toward us as we behave toward him. (Studies show that we experience greater empathy when we put ourselves in the other person's shoes than when we try to imagine *his* feelings.[1]) And communicating to others as we would like them to communicate to us is a valuable exercise in the great art of seeing the other person as the center of his own world.

Considerateness is pragmatic. If we fulfill each other's needs, each of us will want to maintain the relationship with the other, to do business with him, and to please him. If we are honest, reveal our thinking, and are cooperative in our relationships, each of us is more likely to develop genuine communication.

1. Stotland, Ezra, Stanley E. Sherman, and Kelly G. Shaver, *Empathy and Birth Order*. Lincoln: University of Nebraska Press, 1971.

This is supported by a study on the effect of communication on trust. When people played a two-person game that either or both could win or lose depending on their cooperativeness, it was found that the amount of trust was directly related to the amount of communication about intentions and expectations of cooperation. The more the communication, the greater the trust.[2]

Let's consider an example of lack of empathy in conversation:

Bill: What a trip I had! It was unbelievable. The customers must have gotten together to gang up on me this week. And the new motel I tried was a house of horrors.

Tom: I'm glad you're back. I wanted to talk to you about some of these accounts we've been having credit problems with.

Bill wanted to talk about the trouble he had had, but Tom was unresponsive, attuned only to his own needs. So Bill was frustrated in trying to let out his own feelings, perhaps even blocked from working up to a problem he might have wanted to discuss with Tom.

As a result, Tom probably did not have Bill's full attention or his interest. Bill may have sulked a little inwardly while Tom was trying to get through to him. To have been kind, all Tom needed to do was to ask, "What happened?" and listen to Bill sound off.

We have to guard against thinking we don't have time to listen. Believing ourselves in a hurry, we forget how little extra time is required. A few more minutes of responsiveness on Tom's part would have been enough. And for the person who wants large chunks of time, who would use us as long as we're willing to listen, we can at least give a little and then cut it off. We must resist the tendency to give nothing when we feel that the other person will take too much.

One constant need is to make sense out of what confronts us.

2. Loomis, James L., "Communication, the Development of Trust and Cooperative Behavior." *Human Relations,* 1959, Vol. 12, pp. 305–315.

Attaining closure is pleasurable, rewarding; we want to fill in the missing part. As Woodworth has written,

Perception is always driven by a direct, inherent motive which might be called the will to perceive. To see, to hear—to see clearly, to hear distinctly—to make out what one is seeing or hearing— moment by moment, such concrete motives dominate the life of relation with the environment. . . .[3]

This need for closure is illustrated in the story about the music class that decided to play a joke on its professor. Hearing the professor in the hall, approaching the door to the classroom, one of the students played a scale on the piano, omitting the last note of the scale. When the professor entered the classroom he immediately walked to the piano and played the last note of the scale, achieving closure. In a conversation, when we move toward understanding, we are seeking closure.

Ambiguity enters whenever information is incomplete, unreliable, or pointless. Ambiguity causes anxiety in the listener because he feels uncertain how to react. In one experiment, some persons had ambiguous interviews in which no guidance was given as to what to talk about, while others had structured interviews, in which guidance was given. Psychologists' ratings found that anxiety was higher during the ambiguous interviews.[4]

The drive toward closure frequently causes us to jump to conclusions about the other person's goal. Mentally, we race ahead of him, trying to force his meaning and refusing to acknowledge any ambiguities. Similarly, problem-solving and decision-making are achievements of closure, and there is some tension generated when we are short of closure.

In another experiment, people who were made anxious by a threat to their self-esteem tended to form conclusions prema-

3. Woodworth, R. S., "Reenforcement of Perception." *American Journal of Psychology*, 1947, Vol. 60, pp. 119–124.
4. Dibner, A. S., "Ambiguity and Anxiety." *Journal of Abnormal and Social Psychology*, 1958, Vol. 56, pp. 165–174.

turely, to attain closure impulsively. They were first made anxious by being told—untruthfully—that they had done poorly on a test that measures a skill highly related to personal effectiveness and professional success. They were then given an incoherent and unstructured one-paragraph story and asked to interpret it. Rather than admit its incoherence, they forced some meaning from it. No two people gave the same meaning. The people in another group that had not been similarly threatened were more willing to admit that they were uncertain about the meaning of the story.[5]

We must each respond to the other person's desire to attain closure. We need to provide repetition and to ask questions to make sure the other person is receiving all the information so that he can complete the picture accurately. To prevent his jumping to conclusions, we should satisfy the other person's need for closure immediately, telling him right off what we want and what he will gain. We have to keep our remarks brief, feeding in a little information at a time. And we should ask questions that will make our listener consider and grasp the implications of what we are saying.

We also have to empathize with each other's need for approval. When we express approval of others we bolster their feeling of self-esteem. When encountering opposing conclusions in conversation, we need to acknowledge their merits. By doing so, we enable the other person to save face while he comes around to our position. But if we acknowledge merit when it doesn't exist, we lose credibility. And we need to empathize with the other person's feelings of discomfort when he finds himself on the short end of the logic.

While riding once on a bus, I saw a man get out of his seat and stand swaying in the aisle, making comments to the passengers as a group in the typical slurred speech of the drunk. After a few minutes, the driver stopped the bus at the side of the

5. Dittes, James E., "Impulsive Closure as Reaction to Failure-Induced Threat." *Journal of Abnormal and Social Psychology*, 1961, Vol. 63, pp. 562–569.

road. He got up and faced the drunken man, who was about fifteen feet further down the aisle. The conversation between them went something like this:

Driver:	Hey, sit down in your seat. You can't stand in the aisle.
Drunken Man:	(*In slurred, drunken speech*) I don' wanna sit down. I'm gonna stand here.
Driver:	(*In an irritable tone*) You can't stand there. Now, c'mon, take your seat.
Drunken Man:	No, I'm not gonna sit down. I wanna stand here.
Driver:	(*In an exasperated voice*) Listen, you gotta sit down. You stand there an' you're gonna fall down an' break your head, and I'm not gonna be responsible.
Drunken Man:	You don have to be responsible. I'm gonna stand here.

The driver got into his seat, pulled the bus back onto the road, and drove off. As the bus accelerated, the drunken man fell on his back in the aisle. Heavy and bulky, he couldn't seem to coordinate the muscles needed for getting to his feet.

Several of us made ineffectual tugs at his arms in a vain effort to get him up. Then a young fellow knelt down and gently coaxed the drunken man to his feet through a combination of encouraging, sympathetic words and gradual lifting. In soft tones, the young man guided the drunken one toward a seat and gently persuaded him to sit down. The young man then returned to his own seat near the front of the bus and called out angrily to the driver, "You shoulda related." After a few moments, the young man said again, "You shoulda related." And a moment later he said it a third time, as though he were trying to drive his message into the consciousness of the driver, who did not respond, and as though the young man needed to repeat the criticism in order to discharge his obvious anger at the driver.

The driver had his own emotions to contend with. He was probably angry at the drunken man for the interruption (perhaps making him late in completing his scheduled run and getting home), and he was afraid of being responsible for an injury if the drunken man fell. Empathizing, in the face of one's own emotions, requires a determined effort.

The ability to empathize can be developed. If you follow the system of communicating given in this book, a system for opening the conversation and for forming remarks in a specific way, depending upon what the other person says, you will be automatically accommodating for the other person's needs in communicating.

3 Orienting the Other Person's Thinking

The Illusion of Control over the Other Person's Thinking

Whenever we propose an idea, we are faced with the possibility of rejection. This fear pulls us inward, causing us to focus too much on our own thinking and not enough on the other person's. If we have a generalized feeling that people accept us and our ideas, we are likely to be less defensive about the proposal. If we generally doubt our own ideas, we are likely to expect others to doubt them too.

When we fear rejection, we often open a conversation by trying to control the other person's processing of information so that he cannot make a decision until he has received from us all the information we want him to have. We may attempt to do this by "setting the stage," leading up to our proposal with information which we feel will cause him to accept the proposal when we finally make it. But if we want a person to take a certain action for a particular benefit, it is a mistake to begin by telling him about a problem or a need, thinking that when we come to our proposal he will readily accept it. In trying to control someone's mind by feeding him information in a certain order, we defeat ourselves; for we can only control what we say, not what another person is thinking.

Remember: As soon as the other person starts to receive information he tries to orient it, to place it in a larger whole, to relate it, to get the point. From his experiments, Bartlett concluded:

... it is fitting to speak of every human cognitive reaction—perceiving, imaging, remembering, thinking and reasoning—as an *effort after meaning* ... [there is always] an effort to connect what is given with something else ... the immediately present "stands for" something not immediately present.... [We try to relate what we see to something we already know.][1]

People are continually trying to attain closure, to see the whole picture; if we don't supply it, the other person will guess at one and formulate a reaction. Unlike computers, we are not limited to the information the operator gives us.

Consider the boss who wants to tell a supervisor that his subordinates are complaining about his harshness, his tendency to criticize too readily, and his unwillingness to compliment them or to listen to their problems. Suppose the boss wants to suggest that the supervisor be more patient, considerate, and approachable. The boss opens the conversation:

"John, I've been observing your way of dealing with your subordinates and it seems to me that you're too harsh with them, too critical. In fact, some of them have come to me and complained that you never want to listen to them and that you're always criticising them unfairly. They feel that you're never willing to give a compliment."

Hearing this, the supervisor doesn't know where the boss is heading. Is the boss about to fire him, transfer him to a non-supervisory position, or suggest that he change his behavior? If the supervisor thinks he is about to be fired, he might become defensive, justifying his behavior with rationalizations: You have to treat people harshly or they won't work; or these people are just out to get me; or I wasn't harsh at all, it's just that these

1. Bartlett, F. C., *Remembering*. Cambridge, England: Cambridge University Press, 1932, p. 44.

people are too sensitive. His defensiveness will prevent him from being open to change.

Suppose, on the other hand, the boss had begun the conversation in this manner:

"John, I think that if you were to be more patient with your subordinates, would listen to them more and compliment them more often, rather than being so harsh and critical, they'd be more productive and you'd have less turnover of employees, as a result of improved morale. Several of your people have complained to me about your harsh way of dealing with them, and I've observed it also in several instances."

Now there's no question about the boss's intentions. The supervisor knows immediately that he is not going to be fired; the boss just wants him to try a different approach to his subordinates. Not driven to become fearful and defensive, he remains open to suggestions for improvement.

Beginning at the End

Let's consider further the impulse to control another person's thinking. We want him to confine his thoughts to absorbing information as we give it to him, and then to use that information to arrive at our conclusion.

Suppose we want someone to buy a new machine that will do a job more quickly with less labor and maintenance. Instead of coming right out and telling him that we want him to buy this new machine, we may put off stating the whole picture, fearing that he will react negatively to our proposal. Thus we make the mistake of feeding him particular pieces of information in an effort to control his reasoning:

"This old machine of ours is always breaking down and we've been paying out a lot of money for repairs. And with the machine down so much we haven't been able to keep up with our work and we've had to have a lot of overtime, which has cost us a lot of money.

Don't you think we ought to cut down the overtime and repairs on this machine?"

Here we treat the other person as though he were a logic device, able to think only on the basis of information inputs, rather than as a person whose mind moves ahead, trying to grasp the whole picture. Withholding our conclusion, we show our fear that he will not think rationally. Our distrust of him will in turn evoke his distrust of us.

The other person needs to think autonomously. He wants to start with your conclusion and compare it in his own way with available alternatives. He wants to decide for himself what information he needs, and he can do this only if he knows what he needs it for. In keeping our conclusions from the other person, we put him in the position of not knowing our aim. The anxiety arising from the ambiguity confronting him causes him to be suspicious, cautious, and defensive, which works against successful persuasion.

Consider our anxiety that the other person will reject our proposal: If he does say no, does that necessarily end the conversation? Isn't the logical response to no, why not?

If we keep in mind that the purpose of the opening remark is to motivate the other person to continue the discussion, we realize we should start at the end, first giving our conclusions and then exploring his position if he disagrees or giving him more information if he agrees.

One experimental study has demonstrated that making your conclusions explicit results in better comprehension by your listener than does giving him information and letting him draw his own conclusions.[2] Another study, dealing with opinion change rather than comprehension, found that making conclusions explicit, as opposed to letting listeners draw their own conclusions, resulted in twice as many people changing their opinions.[3]

2. Thistlewaite, Donald L., Henry de Haan, and Joseph Kamenetsky, "The Effects of Directive and Nondirective Communication." *Journal of Abnormal and Social Psychology*, 1955, Vol. 51, pp. 107–113.
3. Hovland, Carl I., and Wallace Mandell, "An Experimental Com-

The Golden Rule in Communicating

While we have developed rules of courtesy to make us considerate of the other person's needs, few of these are applied to conversation. We learn ordinary table manners, we learn to share, to return what we've borrowed, and not to malign. But for conversation we haven't learned much about courtesy beyond not interrupting.

Our conversational courtesy does not extend to limiting the information in a remark to what the other person can reasonably absorb at a time. Nor do we reveal our thinking to him so that he can think along with us rather than be used as a source of information, perhaps to be maneuvered into a logical entrapment. We too readily impose on others the discomfort of uncertainty about what we mean. And we make little accommodation for the other person's occasional need to drift mentally.

If we were to use the Golden Rule in communicating, communicating to others as we would like them to communicate to us, communication barriers would be broken and a fuller mutual understanding would be reached more quickly.

Planning the Opening Remark

The Golden Rule tells us immediately that we shouldn't "prepare" the other person for what we want. When someone opens a conversation with us, we want him to come to the point. We don't want to be "prepared."

Suppose you want to persuade your teenage son to keep his room neat and his bed made. And suppose you began by saying:

"I know you want to make a good impression on others, and people make judgments about us from the rooms we live in."

---

parison of Conclusion-Drawing by the Communicator and by the Audience." *Journal of Abnormal and Social Psychology*, 1952, Vol. 47, pp. 581–588.

Since your son does not know how this comment relates to what you are about to tell him, he might jump to various conclusions: You're expecting company imminently and want him to get his room into shape right now; you don't like the decorations on his walls; you think he ought to make his bed and keep his books and records on the shelves; or you are about to discuss ways in which people form impressions of us. Your son's need to attain closure causes him to guess at what you intend to say, and since the conclusion he forms might be less favorable than yours, you might just as well put your own conclusion up front.

The Problem of Clutter

When we're anxious, we tend to clutter our talk. This tendency was demonstrated in an experiment in which a group of people who were highly anxious to begin with, as measured by a test of anxiety, and another group who were made anxious, were compared to a third group low in anxiety to begin with and to a fourth group that was not made anxious. The groups were compared on the basis of how much non-relevant material they included in their answers to questions. One group was made anxious by being told that their answers would indicate how well they would perform in school and at work. The group that was not made anxious was told only that the questions were part of a study of language. Both the group that was highly anxious to begin with and the group made anxious by expecting to be judged by their answers had more irrelevancy in their answers than did both the group with low anxiety to begin with and the group that was not made anxious.[4]

Since the other person is inclined to clutter us with information when he is anxious, he "reads" our anxiety from our clut-

4. Gynther, Ruth A., "The Effects of Anxiety and of Situational Stress on Communicative Efficiency." *Journal of Abnormal and Social Psychology*, 1957, Vol. 54, pp. 274–276.

ter. This communication of anxiety is likely to hinder his receptivity, for it will make him wonder why we are anxious.

Apart from the communication of anxiety, information in cluttered form cannot be absorbed properly; unimportant items may very well crowd out more significant ones.

4 Motivating the Other Person to Listen

Bringing Out the Benefit

The primary purpose of the opening remark should be to motivate the other person to pursue the conversation rather than to take a suggested action. Too many opening remarks, aiming at persuading to action, contain almost the whole presentation, as though the opening remark were the speaker's only chance. When too much information is presented, the listener must either ask the speaker to repeat (which may be awkward); try to infer the information missed (which leaves him uncertain); or mentally withdraw. And too little in an opening remark may not motivate the listener to continue.

What then should the opening remark contain? It should include both our suggested action and the benefit of taking such action. It would be helpful to get into the habit of always thinking of action and benefit as a unity, so that one is always mentioned with the other. If we don't describe the benefit, the listener's drive for closure might move him to supply one from his imagination, and his might be less motivating than ours.

Presenting the Benefit for Greater Impact

The result of taking a suggested action is seldom just a single benefit. It is a cause-and-effect chain of beneficial results, one bringing about another which in turn leads to still others.

Suppose the persuader wants to hire an additional worker because of a backlog of orders. The suggested action is to hire another worker. The immediate result is that more goods are produced. This in turn leads to deliveries being made on time, which results in fewer complaints, which leads to retaining customers who might otherwise be lost. Retaining customers results in more sales, more sales means more profit, more profits provides additional money for investment in marketing and manufacturing, and that leads to still further profit.

The opening remark cannot contain this entire sequence of benefits. It should, however, include the result that will be most persuasive to the other person. If the end result will be closer to the other person's ultimate goal, it will be the most persuasive. As we proceed from hiring an additional person to getting more work done, to clearing up a backlog of orders, to making deliveries on time, to keeping customers satisfied, to making more sales, and finally to making more profit we find that making more profit is much more persuasive than the more immediate results of increased production and on-time deliveries.

Where then do we stop in this chain? The place to stop is at the last result that automatically follows. It automatically follows from the action of hiring an additional person that all the subsequent results, to the end result of making more profit, will occur. However, it doesn't automatically follow that additional profit would be invested in marketing and manufacturing. This introduces another topic and would require further decision-making. And when we introduce new material, we cloud the issue.

Since the end benefit has the greatest persuasive impact, we should include this in the opening remark. But we also need to mention the immediate benefit so the other person will understand how we arrived at the end benefit. If we say merely that we will make more profit by hiring an additional employee, the other person may not see the connection; he might wrongly imagine we want this new employee to call on customers. We must therefore state the immediate benefit of keeping our customers by making deliveries on time through turning out more products. Our opening remark should include, then, the suggested action, the immediate benefit, and the end benefit.

Suppose you are sharing an office with two other people and you want to persuade your boss to put up partitions in order to make smaller individual offices. The suggested action is to put up partitions to make separate offices. The immediate benefit is that there would be fewer distractions from conversations with visitors and on the telephones. The end benefit is that more work could be turned out.

Now, if we combine the three elements, suggested action, immediate benefit, and end benefit, putting end benefit before immediate benefit because the end benefit has greater persuasive impact, the proposal part of the opening remark would sound like this: If we put up partitions to make a separate, small office for each of us, our productivity will increase as a result of fewer distractions from visitors and from phone calls.

It doesn't matter whether the suggested action comes before or after the end benefit, but the immediate benefit should generally be third in the sequence. At times it may come before the suggested action, but it should always come after the end benefit. Here the suggested action came first, but the proposal could have begun with the end benefit: We can increase productivity by putting up partitions to make an individual office for each of us. This will mean fewer distractions from visitors and phone calls.

A housewife wants her husband to pick up an item at a store near his office so that she will be free to take their son ice-skating. She knows that her husband is particularly interested in the boy's learning to skate. The suggested action is: the husband would pick up the item. The immediate benefit is: she could take the son skating. And the end benefit is: the son would improve his skating. Her opening proposal, putting the suggested action first and the end benefit before the immediate benefit, might then be: "If you could pick up the phonograph that we need tonight for Jane's birthday, John would have a chance after school to improve his ice-skating, because I would have time to take him."

Often you will have two separate benefit sequences stemming from the same suggested action. Each can be stated in turn, but the end benefit of each should come before its immediate benefit. A husband says to his wife: "I think we ought to buy a dog. It could save us money and worry because his bark would scare away burglars. It would give the children the great pleasure of having a pet, which they have wanted for years. And they would learn to be responsible for someone else." Here there are three separate lines of benefits: money and worry will be saved in scaring off burglars; the children will enjoy having a pet; and the children will learn to be responsible.

Suppose an executive wants to add a second shift in order to eliminate the high expense of overtime with one shift. His opening proposal might be: "If we put on a second shift, we'll save a lot of money in overtime." The suggested action is to put on a second shift; the end benefit is the saving of a lot of money; and the immediate benefit is eliminating overtime (condensed to "in overtime").

The Question as a Motivator

While the benefit motivates, it does not always prod the other person to think actively. He may still be listening passively, taking in information and wondering where it will lead, not yet reaching out mentally for ways to use the information. He needs to be moved to think constructively and to make a decision. However, since thinking requires effort and decision-making is risky, he may resist doing this.

Therefore, in making our proposal, we should follow it with a question to stimulate the other person to react. A question will point the mind in a specific direction and set it in motion.

A father wants to persuade his son to go to college. The son thinks of taking a job instead. The father's proposal might be: "If you go to college for the next four years, you're likely to spend the following forty years at a more interesting job and have a higher income." While the son may comprehend this proposal, he might not think fully about it. He may instead be tuned in more to his own negative inner feelings. Suppose, however, the father adds a question: "Does it seem worth it to you to spend four years at college if it means working for the rest of your life at a higher income and in a more interesting job?" To answer the question, the son has to think about the proposal.

The son's response to the question is likely to indicate what bothers him most at the moment. He might want to get married or to travel; he might not know what he wants to study; or he might be worried about the financial requirements. The son's reply will tell the father what to discuss. Otherwise the father might dwell on arguments that do not touch on the son's concerns.

A training director proposes to his boss: "We ought to train our managers in persuasion, since persuading is a large part of their job. This could result in more good ideas being implemented and in better-motivated subordinates." The boss might be willing to listen further, but how much more actively would he consider the proposal if the training director added a question that demanded the boss's reaction? To respond, the boss has to focus his thinking. He has to consider his objections, decide what further information he needs, and compare the gains with the costs. The boss's reaction then gives the training director a cue to what he should talk about next. The boss might raise an objection about cost; he might express doubt that the managers would feel that they needed such training; or he might want to know specifically what kind of course the training director had in mind.

In general, a question following a proposal stimulates the other person to think and to communicate his thinking. We can then relate our further thinking to his response.

5 Quantifying Intangibles

Quantifying to Prevent Ambiguity

Our proposal directs the other person toward a weighing of the cost of our suggested action against the gain of its benefit, whether this be in money, time, effort, security, or comfort. And in order to make a weighing he has to have a quantity for each side.

Without values for the suggested action and the benefit, our proposal is ambiguous. Will the benefit outweigh the cost? If it does, by how much? Every investment involves a risk that the outcome will not be as predicted; the benefit has to outweigh the cost by enough to justify the risk. If the other person isn't given any values, he is likely to make them up to eliminate the ambiguity. Even a gut reaction implies quantifying, for if a person responds to a proposal with a quick rejection, it means that he has made some estimates of cost and benefit, even if they were so superficial and quick that he was hardly aware of the effort.

The other person may also form a conclusion about the proposal based on his experience with a similar proposition. However, the differences between the two might be so crucial that his conclusion about the present proposal isn't valid. And if he wants to avoid taking the suggested action because of some feeling such as the fear of making a change, he isn't likely to be too scrupulous about his reasoning. He may then exaggerate the cost and minimize the benefit.

One striking experiment illustrates the distorting of perception by fear. Each subject was shown a rectangle on a screen similar to a television screen. The width of the rectangle was fixed at two inches, but the subject could adjust the height of the rectangle by turning a knob. The subject was shown how to make the rectangle taller by turning the knob to the right and shorter by turning the knob to the left. He was then asked to make the rectangle a square, that is, to make the height equal to the width.

An electrode was attached to the subject's hand that was not being used to turn the knob, and the subject was given an electric shock whenever he adjusted the height below a certain level and reported the figure as being square. By keeping the height above a certain level he could avoid the shock. However, he was not told why or when he was being shocked.

During the experiment it was found that the subjects made the rectangle taller than it should have been for it to be square, in order to avoid an electric shock. Yet at the end of each attempt the subject always perceived the rectangle as square. Further, the subjects believed that there was no way to tell when the shock would be given and that they always succeeded in adjusting the figure to look perfectly square.[1]

Similarly, our fear of taking a suggested action can alter our perception so that we see the benefit as smaller, or our objection as larger, than it really is, without our being aware that our fear causes this distortion. Since people often find ambiguity threatening and will distort their perception to remove a threat, they are likely to assume that we have in mind the quantity that they imagine—if we fail to specify what we do have in mind. When you propose a certain action to save money, and you don't say how much money, the other person is likely to imagine an amount. And if you don't specify the cost of taking the action, he is likely to imagine the cost. He will then base his immediate reaction to your proposal on his weighing of his imagined bene-

1. Solley, Charles M., and Gardner Murphy, *Development of the Perceptual World*. New York: Basic Books, 1960, pp. 245–251.

fit against his imagined cost. This in turn will affect his motivation to pursue the discussion further.

Quantifying to Increase Credibility

Quantifying also increases credibility because it implies that you have done the necessary calculations to come up with the figures. Since your proposal is based on research, rather than on the whim of the moment, the other person is more motivated to listen.

An experiment has found that people find a communicator more trustworthy if he gives supporting evidence for his opinions instead of just stating the opinions.[2] Another study found that good use of evidence increased the listener's view of the speaker as authoritative and produced a greater change in attitude than did poor use of evidence.[3] Listeners do see qualitative differences in evidence; they judge evidence objectively without being largely influenced by initial attitudes and preconceptions.

Suppose you propose that a certain machine be overhauled twice a year to save five thousand dollars a year in production delays that occur because the machine breaks down unexpectedly. The overhaul takes one person two days.

This quantification in the opening remark shows that you have worked out the exact time required for the overhaul procedure, that you have studied the cost of the breakdowns, and that you have determined the proportion of the breakdowns likely to be eliminated by the overhaul. Your having done your homework gives your proposal much greater credibility. And since you have supplied the quantities, the other person cannot insert them from his imagination to serve his own wishes.

The weighing of a five-thousand-dollar saving against the cost of one man's time for two days, twice a year, clearly points to the wisdom of adopting the overhaul procedure. Therefore the

2. Brehm, Jack W., and David Lipsher, "Communicator-Communicatee Discrepancy and Perceived Communicator Trustworthiness." *Journal of Personality*, 1959, Vol. 27, pp. 352–361.
3. McCroskey, James, "The Effects of Evidence in Persuasive Communication." *Western Speech*, Summer 1967, pp. 189–199.

other person can't reject your proposal out of hand without seeming irrational. Even if he doubts your figures or dislikes change or feels that his man will not be able to learn to do an overhaul well enough, he is motivated to pursue the proposal further. To reject it, he has to find some error in your estimates, and to do that, he has to find out more from you. The opening here fulfills the primary purpose of the opening remark: to motivate the other person to want to know more so that he will pursue the discussion.

Making Benefits Measurable

Generally, the suggested action will be easy to quantify. It might simply be the price of something you want to buy, the cost of hiring people for a certain period, or the time it takes to learn a particular task. However, the value of the benefit is more difficult to establish. The benefit is often a mixture of gainful results, some of which can be easily measured while others cannot.

To arrive at the value of a seemingly impossible-to-measure benefit, visualize the scene both before and after the suggested action takes place. Perhaps you want to persuade your boss to overhaul the heating system because it continually breaks down, causing the temperature to drop and making the office workers uncomfortable. Your boss prefers to have the heating system repaired whenever it breaks down; he doesn't want to spend money on a new one or on overhauling the old one. However, it breaks down about every three weeks. Your boss acknowledges that this is an inconvenience, but he claims that nothing is really lost because the employees continue working even though they are cold.

Now, to determine what to quantify in this situation, let's visualize the scene, imagining ourselves among the office workers. The heating system has broken down and the temperature has plummeted. Everybody is cold. What's likely to happen? The employees will complain to each other, joke about the cold, put their coats on, and jump up and down and hug themselves, half to warm up and half to be funny. And all of this takes time away from their work.

Let's estimate that fifteen percent of the employees' time is spent in these unproductive actions. Suppose, too, that for twenty-seven weeks of the year the temperature is low enough to cause discomfort when the heating system breaks down. Since the breakdowns occur on an average of once every three weeks, the office temperature would be uncomfortably cold nine days a year.

If it takes two-thirds of the day, on the average, to repair the heating system, the employees would be uncomfortably cold for the equivalent of six days a year. If four hundred employees are so affected, whose average wage is $35 a day, the loss of fifteen percent of their time for six days a year will amount to $12,600 annually.

It would also be reasonable to expect this periodic freezing to cause some workers to quit. If the normal employee turnover rate increases from ten percent to eleven percent, forty-four persons would leave instead of forty. If it costs $7,000 to re-cruit, screen, hire, train, and subsidize a new employee until he achieves the productivity level of the person leaving, it will cost $28,000 to replace four employees. Adding $28,000 in em-ployee turnover expense to $12,600 in lost employee time amounts to a loss of more than $40,000.

But if the total cost of overhauling the heating system is only $15,000, the benefits which accrue year after year will far out-weigh the cost of taking the suggested action. Since your boss doesn't want to spend the money, he tells himself your proposal isn't worthwhile, and he won't consider it further. But when you quantify, he realizes that his gut reaction may be wrong, and he is motivated to learn more about your proposal.

Suppose a wife wants her husband to spend $500 to convert the pantry on the first floor into a laundry room. The present laundry room is in the basement, and the wife is tired of going up and down the two flights of stairs between the second floor and the basement. She does eight loads of laundry on her weekly washday.

The wife needs to count the number of round trips she makes on washdays and then cut the number in half to find out her saving if she moved the laundry room to the first floor. Then she could amortize the $500 cost over the approximately two hundred and fifty washdays in a five-year period (a conservative estimate of how long they are likely to live in the house).

She might then propose to her husband: "Darling, I've figured out that if we convert the pantry on the first floor into a laundry room, I would have more energy for you and the children and it would be better for my health. It would save me four round trips of two flights of stairs, carrying sixteen pounds of laundry each way, every Monday. To save all this work would cost us only two dollars a week over the next five years. What do you think of converting the pantry to a laundry room if it means my having more energy for you and the kids, and better health, for just two dollars a week?"

The wife has provided the quantities and presented them in perspective. Since, on the face of it, the weighing favors taking the suggested action, the husband will be motivated to explore the situation further. And the housewife's credibility is enhanced by her showing that she has thought through the situation fully. She could have added a further refinement by pointing out, before her question, "I realize that we would lose some interest on the $500 we would have to take out of the bank for this, but we would get this back several times over in the increased value of the house, since a new laundry room on the first floor would be very desirable." This indicates still more extensive thinking by the wife, and the resultant increase in her credibility will motivate her husband to listen even more intently.

Using Measurables Rather Than Abstractions

In order to quantify a benefit we have to pursue the cause-and-effect benefit sequence to the point where the benefit is measurable. We can't stop at a benefit such as improved morale; that is an abstraction which we can't quantify because we don't observe it directly, only its results. But improved morale might result in such measurables as increased production and lower absenteeism and employee turnover. Similarly, you can't quantify the benefit of better communication. You have to carry it forward to such measurable results as fewer errors and less time between an event and the reaction to it. Nor can you measure directly an improvement in training. What you can measure is the change in behavior: the trainee's superior performance of a task.

If we get into the habit of talking in observables and measurables, we not only eliminate the ambiguity that resides in abstractions, but we also give our benefits much greater significance. We are then more persuasive.

Negotiating the Quantification

While it's easier and more comfortable to quantify when we have definite numbers, we need to take the risk of estimating when we don't, if we want to be more persuasive. Ambiguity waits unobtrusively on the edges of our talk, ready to creep in and muddy meaning; we have to be continually vigilant to keep it out.

When we talk about the price of an item, the number of units a machine can turn out per hour, or the percentage of employees who left last year, there are generally definite numbers available, and we should make the effort to get those numbers whenever we want to form a proposal. But we must also judge the cost of getting the numbers. If it will take six hours of research to find a figure that is not crucial, we can settle for a descriptive term. (Here we are quantifying the cost of obtaining a figure and weighing this cost against the benefit of increased persuasiveness.)

Working with definite numbers requires only the effort of finding them and using them. However, working only with estimates increases our anxiety that we may be wrong and that the other person will treat our estimate as a precise valuation and hold us to it. Too often we avoid estimating in order to escape this anxiety.

If we don't have a number, however, our proposal will be much less convincing; and we have the right, even the obligation, to use suppositions. Hypothesizing enables us to try out ideas without the cost of taking action. We can build a bridge or a factory in our imagination and then perform mathematical operations to see if the bridge or the factory is feasible. If we couldn't hypothesize, we would have to build the bridge and the factory in order to find out whether they would work.

To maintain credibility while gaining the increased persuasiveness of quantifying, we should estimate conservatively and, wherever possible, develop a rationale for our estimates. Don't pick a number out of the air; if the other person discovers that our number came from our imagination, he may dismiss our whole proposal. And when we estimate, we should say so.

One useful device in estimating is to determine how great the benefit would have to be to make the cost worthwhile. Such an estimate might sound like this: "If we increased production by only one percent, it would pay for the cost three times over. And we might very well increase production by five or ten percent."

It's often helpful to involve the other person in the estimating so that he then commits himself either to our estimate or to some adjustment of it. When we negotiate the estimate with the other person, we are likely to wind up using either his estimate or an agreed-upon, in-between figure. In any case, we will then have his commitment.

Let's consider an example of estimating intangible benefits. Suppose we are considering proposing a flexible work-time schedule wherein employees are permitted to choose their hours of work for half of their workday, making this choice on a day-to-day basis. Of their eight working hours a day they would work four hours at the set time of 10 A.M. to 3 P.M. (with an hour off for lunch), and they could then choose their additional four hours from the periods 7 A.M. to 10 A.M. and 3 P.M. to 9 P.M.

One benefit is that employees would work at a higher motivational level since they would be choosing half their hours of work at the time that best suits them—some people work better in the morning, others in the evening—and they would be less distracted by personal business since they could adjust any working day to take care of it. Another benefit is the saving of employee time since they wouldn't all be crowding the parking lot at the same hours.

The losses also have to be estimated. People who normally consult with each other, or take incoming calls during working hours, may not always be available outside the 10 A.M. to 3 P.M. period.

To estimate the costs, we might make a survey of how many phone calls and consultations would be missed, and of the efforts required to educate people to arrange their consultation and calling times during the mandatory work hours or by prior arrangement during the optional work periods. Analysis might show that within two months everyone should have adjusted to the flexible work schedule.

In estimating the benefit, a five percent increase in productivity as a result of increased motivation and a five percent decrease in employee turnover as a result of raised morale might serve as starting points. If each employee saves five minutes in parking his car, the decrease in irritation might also improve his motivation.

The five percent increase in employee productivity could be quantified by considering it the equivalent of a five percent increase in time worked, since the employee would now be doing five percent more work in the same time. One way of quantifying this would be to multiply the number of employee-hours by the average wage per hour and take five percent of this as the benefit. The value of a five percent decrease in employee turnover could be calculated from the cost of hiring an employee and bringing him to the point of development attained by the average of the employees who leave each year.

In using estimates, because there is so much risk that they may be wrong, the benefit will have to outweigh the cost to a much greater extent than if definite figures were being used. If you make a proposal using estimates in which the benefit doesn't exceed the cost by a significant margin (depending on how tenuous the basis for the estimate), you'll lose credibility.

Quantifying is a powerful tool; even an estimated figure has far greater impact than an adjective. So by all means let's estimate, but let's do it conservatively and maintain our credibility. And let's enhance that credibility by negotiating the estimate with the other person.

6 Preventing Misunderstanding

Listening Is Intermittent

No matter how hard we try, we have only limited control over our ability to listen. Our attention is restless, distracted by things around us and by inner preoccupations. Suddenly, we realize we've tuned out, missing information. We turn our attention back and find, with relief, that we're able to pick up the thread of the conversation.

After a little, we become aware that we have lost touch again, and we make an effort to refocus on what the other person is saying. Our attention is elusive; it slips away from the conversation without our noticing. While we can always bring it back, we can't always hold it there.

Our minds dart and flit while reading as well. How often do you find yourself having to reread a paragraph because your mind wandered as you read? Even when motivation is high, our attention is slippery enough to steal away. How often are you introduced to someone and then can't recall his name a moment later? Though it was important to learn the name to avoid the embarrassment of asking for it again, your attention wasn't cooperating.

Try to hold the letter "T" in your mind. After less than 30 seconds your attention is likely to be somewhere else, and you'll have to make an effort to bring it back to the "T"—only to find a short time later the "T" is no longer there.

Losing the Thread of Meaning

When our attention drifts briefly and then returns, we are able usually to pick up the thread of the other person's meaning. What we missed was not enough to prevent us from connecting up because our way of talking has some repetition built into it.

If we were to speak telegraphically, cramming a maximum of information into a minimum of words, we would lose each other quickly; even a few seconds' lapse in our attention would cause us to lose too much. Even with the redundancies in our conversations, every so often our attention drifts a little too long, and when we tune in again we can't follow what the other person is saying. An experiment found that when a single word is deleted from a sentence only twelve words in length, the listener replaces that word correctly only fifty percent of the time, and he has just a seventy-five percent chance of getting the meaning intended by the sentence.[1]

Sometimes a speaker condenses his remarks so much that we miss too much information when we are in the out phase of our tuning in and out. We might miss a key idea, and when we return to the in phase, we're unable to connect what's being said with what we heard just before we tuned out.

Asking for Missed Information

When an information gap develops because our attention was elsewhere, we can ask the other person to repeat, we can guess at what he said, or we can let him talk on, hoping he will supply the missing information. The surest way to fill the information gap correctly is to ask the other person to repeat what we missed.

We may be reluctant to ask this, for it reveals that we weren't listening; actually, we have no reason to be embarrassed—

1. Morrison, H. M., and J. W. Black, "Prediction of Missing Words in Sentences." *Journal of Speech and Hearing Disorders*, 1957, Vol. 22, pp. 236–240.

tuning out is inevitable and familiar to everyone. It is a common illusion that the maintaining of attention is purely voluntary, that if the listener's attention wanders, it means that he is bored. If we understand the limited control we have over our attention, we can all ask freely for missed information without embarrassment.

Repeating to Accommodate
for Tuning Out

There is not enough repetition built into our way of talking to allow for the amount of tuning out that goes on. If a light bulb went on above your head each time you tuned out, you'd be amazed at the size of your electric bill.

Repetition must be unobtrusive. If repetition is obvious, the listener will find the conversation slow and dull and will tune out more often. Repeating will then increase the loss of information. How then does one repeat without being dull? One general rule is to avoid using words or phrases that refer to something you said before. Instead of using *it* or *that*, or such phrases as *this way of doing it* and *the plan I talked about*, repeat the subjects those words or phrases stand for.

After speaking of your need to hire another man because of increased work, you want to add that you've discussed this with your boss. Rather than say, "I talked to my boss about *it*," say, "I talked to my boss about *hiring another man*." Repeating the subject, rather than using words that only refer to it, will help fill the gaps that occur when the other person tunes out.

As we talk, we need to be aware that until we get feedback, we have no way of knowing what the other person has taken in or lost. Asking questions to get feedback is a good way to find out what the other person has absorbed. The question that follows the proposal in the opening remark prevents information loss in three ways: 1) it provides an opportunity for repeating the suggested action and its benefit; 2) it prods the other person to absorb the proposal in order to respond to the question; and

3) it elicits a response that will indicate what the listener has absorbed, allowing any information loss to be corrected.

Summarizing and using visual aids when appropriate are other valuable ways of repeating.

The Value of the Other Person's Talking

Thinking aloud is a common and useful way of developing an idea. As we talk out our ideas we get a clearer view of them. Therefore, why not try to get the other person to talk about our ideas in order to get him to understand them more fully? His talking about our ideas is as important to his absorbing them as is our explaining them to him. When we talk about our ideas he may not be listening; when he talks about them he is taking them in.

We tend to underestimate the value of the other person's talking. His talking is a vital part of his listening. But because we see his talking as the opposite of his listening, we shatter his absorbing process by interrupting him. When he is talking about the ideas we have just presented and he makes a mis-statement, we are too quick to correct him, too anxious to take the explaining away from him and to put it our way.

Doing this, we disrupt his listening and prevent him from building his own mental picture of our idea. For even if there is some error in his conception, it is much better to let him continue to the end of his remark. We can then make the correction after he has finished. This allows him to build a total picture of what we mean, rather than leave it unassembled.

And being interrupted is frustrating. The other person wants to express himself and attempts to build a thought-structure. If you knock it down before he can finish it, he might mentally withdraw from the conversation.

In an experiment to determine the effects of interruption, people learned a sequence of seven words. Each person was told one word at a time at three-second intervals and was asked during the interval to anticipate the next word before it was spoken. The sequence was repeated without interruption; after the seventh word and the three-second interval following it, the first word was spoken again.

Each person continued until he could anticipate each of the seven words without error. Then he was given the word sequence with the last word changed, so that his anticipation was interrupted. The original sequence was then repeated six more times. Now the subject made errors in anticipating words, his thinking disrupted as a result of the interruption. He was also aroused emotionally by the interruption, as indicated by an increase in the electric current flowing over the surface of his skin (a widely used method of evaluating emotional arousal).[2]

Putting ideas into spoken words can be quite pleasurable. We readily see this in the delight that children take in uttering words when they first learn to speak. A person's talking not only gives him the satisfaction of forming ideas and seeing them more clearly, it also enables him to express feeling, which is in itself enjoyable. Consequently, each of us is continually motivated to take away the talking from the other person.

When another person has an appetizing tidbit of food on his fork, we certainly wouldn't stop that fork and take the tidbit for our own mouth. Yet how often do people interrupt others to finish their sentences for them? We have to control both our greed for talking and our anxiety about being misunderstood, to give the other person a chance to finish his remarks. His talking about our ideas will both cause our ideas to take hold in his mind and make the conversation more pleasurable for him.

2. Mandler, George, "The Interruption of Behavior." In Levine, D. (ed.), *Nebraska Symposium on Motivation, 1964*. Lincoln: University of Nebraska Press, 1964, pp. 163–219.

7 Probing for Premises

Losing Touch with Each Other's Thinking

If we view conversation as simply an alternation of self-expression wherein each participant takes a turn talking, we're not likely to achieve a meeting of minds. In this kind of conversation, each person talks to himself and allows the other person to listen. And each maintains the illusion that identical thought structures are forming in both minds.

In a persuasive conversation, the speaker's expectation that parallel thinking is occurring in the listener's mind rests on several assumptions: that the listener is tuned in and thinking; that the speaker's words have the same meaning for both of them; that the listener's preconceptions and personal wishes are not interfering with his reception of the message; that the listener accepts the truth of all the information; and that the listener has absorbed everything presented. Making these unwarranted assumptions, the speaker focuses his attention on his own arguments; if his reasoning appears to him sound and clearly expressed, he concludes that the listener is convinced.

Our faith in what's going on in the other person's mind is particularly acute when we encounter an objection. If the other person protests, "It's too complicated," we respond, "It's not complicated at all. Let me show you how simple it is." Assuming that we know what the other person means by "too complicated," we make our own interpretation of his words. But when he says it's too complicated, does he mean that it's too intricate to master conceptually, that it will take too much time, that too many people are involved, or something else altogether? And how complicated is too complicated? His idea of the point at which something passes from complicated to too complicated may be different from ours.

If someone objects to an action we propose, "It's too expensive," our tendency (if we disagree) is to respond, "It's not expensive. In fact, for what we're getting, it's quite inexpensive." Contradicting him, we make assumptions about the figure he has in mind and his criterion for "too expensive," and then we argue against our own assumptions. When we do this we are talking to ourselves.

Listen to two people in conversation, each assigning his own meanings to the remarks of the other:

"This is a great idea, and it's really going to do a lot for us."
"It won't work."
"Of course it'll work. I covered every angle."
"Too many things could go wrong. There are too many loopholes."
"Nothing's going to go wrong. I tell you I checked it over from every angle and it's perfect. I even ran it through two other guys and they agreed with me."
"We've got to sink too much money into it for what we get out of it. It's too risky. You have to weigh the return against the risk."
"There's very little risk, so stop exaggerating."

In this alternation of claim and counterclaim, no one asks for the evidence underlying the other's reasoning. Each makes his own assumptions. But what are the criteria for whether the plan works? What are the loopholes? How were the angles checked? What could go wrong? How much money would be invested? How much would be returned? What is the risk? Since each knows that his own underlying reasoning is only being guessed at by the other, each will doubt that the other's answers are related to his own concerns.

Reconstructing the Other
Person's Reasoning

We can't answer another person's objection until we understand his reasoning. Suppose someone tells us, "I can't do that. My people wouldn't like it. There would be too much of a fuss." It's too risky to respond without further inquiry because we don't know what he means. His statement is defined only by the reasoning behind it.

If we had answered on impulse, "They'll like it once they realize how much time it will save them," we would have been making our own decision about what was most important to them. In doing this, we run the risk of being wrong, and we create the impression that having our own way is more important than making a sound decision.

Instead we have to make visible, and examine together, the other person's chain of reasoning. His conclusion that he can't do it is based on his premises that his people won't like it and that they will make a fuss. These premises are themselves conclusions based on other premises. We must bring out these prior premises with such questions as: Why won't they like it? To what extent? Will they come to like it when they discover the benefits? Can modifications be made to help them like it? How much of a fuss will they make? Is the other person overreacting to the threat of fuss?

Penetrating the Gut Reaction

Often the other person doesn't have a clear picture of his own underlying thinking; his response might be only a gut reaction. As you have suggested your idea and stopped talking, the other person may speak, simply because he feels the need to give some response. Such an immediate reaction may be based on preconceptions, on experiences that only seem to be similar, and on the emotions. Yet this reaction seems quite logical to the person making it. He feels that, if need be, he can readily produce a sound, logical basis for his response.

In an experiment in which people were required to choose the valid conclusion, reasoning from given premises, it was found that the personal opinions, wishes, fears and convictions of the individual contribute about 35 percent of the deciding influence in choosing the conclusion from the choices given. Actually, logic exerted only about a fifth of the deciding influence, while the form in which the premises and conclusions were expressed contributed a fourth, and chance about a fifth.[1]

Another force behind a person's objection might be his dealing with a problem in a particular way quite different from that which you propose. He might have become habituated in his method, his mind closed to other approaches.

This development of a mental set was demonstrated in a rigorous research study in which people were given a series of problems wherein all the earlier problems were solved by a particular procedure. Using this same procedure to solve problem after problem produced a mental set.

The participants continued to use the same approach throughout the series, even though some of the later problems could be solved in a much more direct and simpler manner. The people clung to the more complicated method they had used in earlier problems, not seeing the easier way. Then, when they were given a problem that could be solved only in the simpler, more direct way, they had difficulty solving it.

The study also found that imposing psychological stress caused the participants to cling still more to their habituated method and to avoid trying new ones. The study further showed that two people working together on problems, communicating their ideas to each other, had greater flexibility, less clinging to the habituated method, and greater success in problem-solving requiring a shift to a new method, than did people working alone.[2]

1. Morgan, J. J. B., and J. T. Morton, "The Distortion of Syllogistic Reasoning Produced by Personal Convictions." *Journal of Social Psychology*, 1944, Vol. 20 (2), pp. 39–59.
2. Luchins, Abraham S., and Edith H. Luchins, *Rigidity of Behavior*. Eugene: University of Oregon Books, 1959, pp. ix, 622.

Motivating the Other Person
to Ask for Your Ideas

When people object spontaneously to a proposal, they are generally unaware that their objection may be a mixture of hard information, assumptions, preconceptions, emotions, inhibiting mental sets, and past beliefs and prejudices. If they could be shown that perhaps they don't know enough about the proposal to evaluate it, that their rejection might have an irrational basis, and that there could be worthwhile benefits for them, they would probably want to know more about the proposal. Therefore, it's most important to turn the other person from a feeling of opposition to a realization that he doesn't know.

This was demonstrated in an experimental study that compared two groups of people for the amounts they learned from instruction. One group contained those who had previously given wrong answers on a pre-test; the other group was made up of those who gave "don't know" answers. A test given to both groups after instruction showed that the people who had previously given "don't know" answers learned better than the people who had previously given wrong answers.[3]

When we encounter an objection, we need to draw the other person out, to ask questions about his underlying thinking, both to understand his reasoning so that we can answer it and to help him examine his own reasoning. If he sees that his substantiation is less strong than he thought it was, he will be motivated to find out more about our thinking. After all, he won't want to reject our idea and its benefits without sufficient reason.

The other person's objection, or statement of disagreement, is our cue to draw him out, to reconstruct and examine his underlying thinking.

3. Doby, John T., "Some Effects of Bias on Learning." *Journal of Social Psychology*, 1960, Vol. 51, pp. 199–209.

8 Asking the
Right Questions

To change another person's conclusions we must first understand and then change his premises.

The other person's support for his objection is often an amalgam of present knowledge and prior beliefs and prejudices sustained and strengthened by his selective processing of information. Psychological studies show that people expose themselves to, pay more attention to, perceive, and remember information that agrees with their prior beliefs.[1] This does not mean that no contrary information is absorbed; it does mean that more of the information that supports their prior beliefs will be absorbed and given greater value.

Other psychological studies show that people, in evaluating reasoning, make mistakes that are in line with their own biases. In one study on reasoning almost twenty percent more mistakes were made when the person's biases were in conflict with his judgment.[2]

At the same time, people need to feel reasonable. This helps us gain access to each other when we are trying to change each other's thinking.

1. Barker, Larry L., and Robert J. Kibbler (eds.), *Speech Communication Behavior.* Englewood Cliffs, N.J.: Prentice-Hall, 1971, pp. 171–173.
2. Mortensen, C. David, *Communication: The Study of Human Interaction.* New York: McGraw-Hill, 1972, pp. 196–199.

The Need to Feel Rational

Without our rationality we would not survive. Generalizations enable us to reason what will happen if certain actions are taken. Through quick, hardly realized applications of logic, we know which moves will result in our winning and which in our losing; and when we're not sure, we know how to weigh probabilities.

Our healthy respect for the survival value of our rationality is shown in our search for reasons to justify what we do. When we act on impulse, out of lust, fear, anger, guilt, or greed, we rationalize to hide from ourselves and from others our real motivations. For we know that impulse can be a dangerous and seductive enemy, leading us into irrationality, possibly to chaos and destruction. (Rationality versus irrationality can be viewed as another face of the core duality, variously expressed as good and evil, love and hate, life and death, and order and chaos.)

In spite of our continually striving to be rational, our messages to each other often become distorted or blocked as they work their way through layers of our irrationality. We tend to misinterpret or reject information when it conflicts with our preconceptions or when its implications are unpleasant to us. We form opinions without sufficient basis, reject soundly supported ideas because they are unpalatable, and look away from reality when it threatens us.

In an interesting study demonstrating the need to feel rational, the same persuasive message was given to two different audiences. To one audience the message was introduced by, "Isn't it only logical that—," while the other audience was given the identical speech without these introductory words. The speech that contained the introductory words appealing to the need to feel logical produced greater persuasion.[3]

The need to feel rational can be a powerful force helping us to reach each other through reason. We might enlist this force by helping the other person to focus his reason on his own underlying thinking before we ask him to consider our thinking.

3. Ibid.

Enlisting the Other Person's
Need to Feel Rational

Persuading the other person to examine his own underlying reasoning will move him toward discovering the irrational elements in that reasoning. If we can get him to question the basis of his objections and the truth of his premises, he will be motivated to find out more about our thinking. As he senses the holes in his thinking, he looks for something sounder to replace his objections.

The uncertainty he feels when he finds weaknesses in his underlying reasoning moves him to ask for information. He becomes more open to our ideas. This was demonstrated in an experiment in which people had to make decisions under varying degrees of uncertainty but were allowed to lessen uncertainty by requesting information. It was found that the tendency to seek information increased with increasing feelings of uncertainty.[4]

The examination of underlying reasoning should be a joint action. We need to know what aspect of our idea bothers the other person so that together we can concentrate on that.

When the other person raises an objection, the general rule is to respond with a question. This may be the first in a series of questions, for you must continue to probe until you reconstruct the other person's underlying reasoning. If he answers your question but still maintains his objection, perhaps explaining it a little more, continue to ask questions until you either agree with his reasoning or see that you have created a condition of uncertainty in the other person.

In an experiment it was found that uncertainty increases only for people who change their judgments (as compared to those who don't change). People were asked to make repeated judgments (of the number of bomb craters in a photograph after brief visual exposures of the photograph), and to express their

4. Driscoll, James M., Jerome J. Tagnoli, and John T. Lanzetta, "Choice Conflict and Subjective Uncertainty in Decision-Making." *Psychological Reports*, 1966, Vol. 18, pp. 427–432.

degree of certainty about their judgments. During the course of exposures the photograph was changed, as was feedback about their performance, without their knowing it. Also, when there is low initial uncertainty, the uncertainty increases markedly when there is a change in judgment. This supports the value of increasing the other person's uncertainty when you are trying to change his opinion.[5] Don't provide information until he asks for it. When he does, either as a question or as an expression of interest in your thinking, give him information.

Remember: Find out *first* the cause-and-effect relationship the other person has in mind, the *why* of what he is saying. What does he base his objection on?

Suppose we propose that our boss undertake a project that could save the company $50,000 a year. In the opening remark we mention this as the quantified end benefit. He replies, "We can't do it. We've got too many other things going." We don't know the cause-and-effect relationship between the "too many other things" and not doing this project, so we must come back with a question.

Let's call this inquiry, one that gets at the cause-and-effect relationship between objection and proposal, a *why* question, whether or not it has the word "why" in it. For example, two equivalents of "why do you think" are "how did you arrive at the conclusion that" and "what makes you think that."

One form of a *why* question here might be, "In what way do these other things prevent us from doing this project?" If we were closely involved on a day-to-day basis with such a situation, it might not be necessary to ask this question; instead, we could go directly to the next question. Other questions here might be: How does this project compare in value with the least valuable of these other projects? How much money (time, people, equipment, etc.) do you think this project will require? The questions to be raised depend on the objections raised by our boss and the premises behind them.

5. Zajonc, Robert B., and Julian Morrissette, "The Role of Uncertainty in Cognitive Change." *Journal of Abnormal and Social Psychology*, 1960, Vol. 61 (2), pp. 168–175.

Questioning the other person about his reasoning requires tact. He may come to feel that his judgment is being doubted or that he has made a mistake and will be embarrassed. He might resent our scrutinizing his thinking and his having to justify it. Therefore, in drawing out his reasoning, our *draw-out remark* should contain, in addition to a question, some provision for easing any discomfort the question might cause.

These ameliorating parts of the draw-out remark should also contain information. Since the question itself is a demand for information, our giving something in return softens the effect of the question. One part of this input should acknowledge whatever is true, possibly true, or plausible in the other person's objection; this will reassure him that we are taking into account his concerns in maintaining our proposal and encourage him to reciprocate by looking at our side as we look at his. We'll call this part of the draw-out remark the *acknowledgment*.

The usefulness of the acknowledgment is shown in an experiment that found that, in conversation, the rate of expressing opinions by one person is increased when the other person agrees with the opinions or paraphrases them, and diminishes when the other person disagrees or does not respond.[6] Another study found that people who indicate agreement with those they're trying to persuade—agreement on at least some ideas, even when these ideas are irrelevant—are likely to be more persuasive.[7]

The input part of the draw-out remark should also include *our* reasoning. Here we can tell why we're asking the question and why we think the answer could be helpful. If we have evidence that contradicts his objection, we should reveal it. Then he will know that we want to check his reasoning against our own in order to determine whether our conclusion is justi-

6. Verplanck, William S., "The Control of the Content of Conversation by Reinforcement of Statements of Opinion." *Journal of Abnormal and Social Psychology*, 1955, Vol. 51, pp. 668–676.

7. Barker, Larry L., and Robert J. Kibler (eds.), *Speech Communication Behavior*. Englewood Cliffs, N.J.: Prentice-Hall, 1971, p. 243.

fied by our evidence. He may have information that we don't have; or there may be some error in our reasoning. If our question is aimed at finding out whether we are thinking along the same lines, we could explain that we want to make sure that both of us have the same thing in mind. This part of the draw-out remark is *the reason for the question*. Stating the reason for the question helps the other person to understand that we are trying to arrive at the best decision and not just trying to win an argument.

The draw-out remark, then, is always used in response to the other person's objecting, that is, to his answering with disagreement or opposition, and is aimed at bringing out the reasoning behind the objection. The draw-out remark consists of a question, which is its essential part; an acknowledgment of something true, possibly true, or plausible in the other person's objection; and a reason for asking the question.

Generally, the acknowledgment is given first, the question is then asked, and, finally, the reason for the question is given. This order has the advantage of providing the giving of information both before and after the request for information. The disadvantage of putting the question first is that so much information then follows it that the other person may forget that a question was asked. And the disadvantage of putting it last is that so much information then comes before the question that the other person might tune out before you get to the question.

Here's a draw-out remark, conforming to this structure, that might be used in response to the other person's objection, "We can't do it. We've got too many other things going":

"It's true, we are into a lot of other things and that does make this difficult. Could you tell me what specifically we're lacking that prevents us from working this in? Maybe we could make some adjustment or find some way of dealing with it."

Now, suppose the other person says, "We can't spare that many people. We would have to pull them off other projects, and those projects are pretty hot right now." This tells us that the specific obstacle in his mind is the delaying of other projects.

To form our next remark we have to decide whether to draw out further information from him or to feed it in. If he is still objecting, we have to draw out further; if he is requesting information, we have to feed in. Actually, although he has explained a little, he is still objecting.

In preparing our next draw-out remark, what question should we ask? The other person objected that too many people would have to be taken off other projects. How many is too many? Isn't it possible that the number of people he has in mind is greater than would be required? Whenever the other person uses a descriptive term in his objection, this is our cue to use a quantifying question in our next draw-out remark. We should now ask a *how much* question, one that gets at quantity.

Here is a form of the next draw-out remark that might be used. It includes an acknowledgment, a quantifying question, and a reason for the question:

"Yes, we would have to take some people off other projects. How many people were you thinking we would need for this project? The reason I ask is, perhaps we can get by with less than you had in mind."

Let's suppose that the other person replies, "It seems to me you'll need three or four people for a project like that, and I just can't spare them. I know your project has merit. But we just can't push aside these other projects right now."

In forming our response, do we continue with another draw-out remark or do we feed in information? To decide this we have to ask ourselves whether the other person is still objecting or whether he is requesting information. The other person is still objecting. He has merely explained his objection further. He expects that we want three or four people from other projects, and on this basis he could not allow the project to be done. Since he is still objecting we have to continue to draw him out. He has not requested information.

Employing the Hypothetical Question

Now we come to the use of the hypothetical, or *what if* question. This is employed when we want to try to change one of the other person's premises or to introduce a new premise, to see if this affects his conclusion. To use the hypothetical question, we first have to discover a premise that we can consider changing.

From the conversation in our example, we have discovered that the boss's premises are that the project will require three or four people; that these people would have to be taken from other projects; that taking them from other projects would hold up the other projects; and that the other projects cannot be held up. From these premises, his conclusion is that this project cannot be done.

But suppose that instead of three or four people we need only two. This means that one of his premises is wrong. Now we want to find out whether changing this premise will also cause him to change his conclusion that the project can't be done.

Our next draw-out remark includes an acknowledgment, a hypothetical question, and a reason for the question, in that order:

"I can certainly appreciate your not wanting to go along with this project if we had to take three or four people off other projects. But what if I could get by with only two people? I think I can manage with two if I get the right people."

Now the other person may reply, "Two people sounds like a possibility. I like the project. Which two people did you have in mind?" He is no longer objecting. He has even asked a question. Our drawing-out sequence opened him up and motivated him to seek information. He has given a cue for a feed-in remark.

In drawing out the other person's objection in order to uncover his underlying reasoning, we would not necessarily use all three kinds of questions, nor need we use them in the same order as we did here. If after our first or second draw-out remark, the other person had asked a question, we would have responded with a feed-in remark to give him the information he requested. On the other hand, if he still maintained his objection after our third draw-out remark, we would have continued to draw him out until he requested information.

Our three draw-out remarks posed three questions: the first contained a question to get at the cause-and-effect relationship between the other person's objection and our proposal ("Could you tell me what specifically we're lacking that prevents us from doing this project?"); the second contained a quantifying question ("How many people were you thinking we would need for this project?"); and the third draw-out remark contained a hypothetical question ("What if I could get by with only two people?").

In bringing forth the thinking behind any other objection, our draw-out remarks would include whatever questions are appropriate for uncovering the other person's reasoning at that particular point. The draw-out sequence does not contain any pre-set order of questions or number of draw-out remarks; you might continue to use the same kind of question in one draw-out remark after another. The kind of question you ask is determined by what the other person has just said and by what particular information you want. In general, your questions will be one of three kinds: *why, how much*, and *what if*.

Another example: A nurse in a hospital is trying to persuade a ten-year-old boy to get out of bed and walk down the corridor and back in order to get some exercise. It would be his first such walk after abdominal surgery. But the boy's reply is, "No, I can't. I don't want to."

The boy's remark is an objection, and the nurse has to control her impulse to respond, "Sure you do. It'll be good for you. You'll get better so much faster." This would be an input of information, but because the boy is objecting, the nurse must respond with a draw-out remark.

Since the nurse doesn't know the reason for the boy's refusal, she should start with a *why* question. She might construct her draw-out remark to include both an acknowledgment and a reason for her question, as well as the question itself:

"I know it seems difficult to you, but why don't you want to try it? If you would tell me what you're thinking, maybe I could find some way to make it feel easier for you."

The boy answers, "I'm afraid it's going to hurt bad if I walk." Now the nurse must decide whether to feed in information or to draw it out. The boy is still objecting; he has merely explained his objection further. He hasn't asked for information. Therefore, the nurse cannot feed in. She has to hold back on telling the boy that it won't hurt and must instead bring to light more of his underlying thinking. She might continue:

"I can understand your being afraid it's going to hurt more since it did hurt some after the operation. But how do you know that walking will make it hurt bad when you haven't even tried to walk? It could even make you feel better."

To illuminate the boy's underlying thinking, the nurse has used two draw-out remarks in a row that contained *why* questions. She was trying to bring out more fully the *because* of his not wanting to walk.

Suppose the boy responds, "I just know it will, and anyway I might fall down and get hurt." The answer, "I just know it will," indicates that he doesn't have a logical reason. His awareness of this causes him to feel that he can't really hold to this position on such a tenuous basis, so he shifts to another concern, "and anyway I might fall down and get hurt."

From what the nurse hàs uncovered, let's reconstruct his reasoning. His premises are: I am weak from my operation; when one is weak one is in danger of falling down; if one falls down, one is likely to get hurt. And implicit in what the boy has said is: I won't be holding on to anything to make sure I won't fall.

To change the boy's conclusion that he will fall, by changing his premise that he won't be holding on to anything, the nurse might now use a *what if* question. First she acknowledges, then asks the question, and then gives a reason for her question:

"Feeling weak the way you do, you probably would feel a little afraid of falling. What if you were to hold on to me while you walked, would you then be willing to try it? You wouldn't have to be afraid of falling, and you could get the exercise that will make you feel better."

The boy replies, "Do I have to walk all the way down to the end of the hall?" The boy's question is the cue for the nurse to feed in information. The drawing-out sequence by the nurse has caused the boy to open his mind and to want to explore the situation further. His objection has been dissipated.

Each of the nurse's three draw-out remarks contained: an acknowledgment of something true, possibly true, or plausible in the boy's objection; a question to bring out his underlying thinking; and a reason for the question. The acknowledgment came first, followed by the question, and then the reason for the question.

9 Feeding In Ideas

Giving Information Only When It's Requested

When persuading another, it is best to provide information only when requested. It is then that the other person is open and receptive. The question, or a statement of interest or agreement, is your cue to begin.

The advantage of feeding in thinking only when the other person asks for it (and drawing out his thinking when he disagrees) was demonstrated in an experiment comparing the mental organization of a person transmitting information with that of a person receiving information. It was found that the person transmitting organized his thinking more specifically, with relationships among ideas more fully worked out, than did the person receiving. Because the receiver didn't know specifically what was coming, he kept his thinking more loosely organized, in broader categories, so that he could better assimilate the information as it came in.

In another part of the experiment, when a group of people were told, before they communicated, that they each would be communicating with someone in another group, who disagreed with them on a judgment based on the same data (whether to hire a particular job applicant), it was found that the receiver was more structured, more specific, more organized in his thinking. He then resembled the transmitter in having a high degree of specificity and organization. But because the organization of his own thinking was too fully worked out, he could not receive the transmitter's information as readily.[1]

It is therefore inefficient to feed in information when the other person disagrees. His mind is not ready to assimilate new information; it is too highly structured, with too many specifics, around his own position. But when he has been brought to a position of wanting to know more, which may be indicated by his asking for information, he has become mentally tuned in. He is then ready to accommodate a new idea structure because his own thinking is looser, less organized, less specific, more ready for change.

The opening remark in a conversation is an exception to the rule of feeding in information only when it is requested. However, it is a special case. It supplies information, orients the receiver to the subject, and lays out the proposal. Since the other person doesn't know what's going to be proposed, he doesn't as yet have any position; and since he has presumably agreed to have a conversation, he will be open to finding out what it is about.

Answering Questions Directly

When the other person asks a question, he is seeking information to help him make a decision. We want to make sure that he builds our answer into his thinking. To do this, we must present the information in a particular way, one that responds most directly to the intent of his question.

There is often a conflict between the way the other person wants to receive information and the way we want to present it. Suppose we want to replace an item of equipment with a newer model that would save employee time. Explaining the advantages of this to the person who has to approve the purchase, we neglect to state the price. He asks, "How much does it cost?"

---

1. Zajonc, Robert B., "The Process of Cognitive Tuning in Communication." *Journal of Abnormal and Social Psychology*, 1960, Vol. 61 (2), pp. 159–167.

Although we know the price, we reply, "It's a little higher than the model we have, but it's well worth it considering all the things it'll do." In this way, we are answering not the question he asked, but the question "How does the price of the more versatile model compare with the price of the model we are using?"

But if we consider the intent of his question, we realize that he wants to know the price so that he can decide whether the extra features are worth the actual difference in cost. Telling him that the price is a little higher, we aren't giving him enough information for him to decide. When we answer a question different from the one asked, the other person is likely to infer that we don't want to answer his question, that either we don't know the answer and don't want to admit it or else the answer is unfavorable for our position. Immediately, the other person becomes suspicious.

Often we frustrate the other person by answering other questions before we come to his question instead of feeding in information in a sequence that gives him first what he wants to know first. Suppose we want to persuade someone to advertise in a magazine other than the one he is now using. We tell him he will get a greater return on his advertising dollar. He asks, "How does the circulation of this magazine compare with that of the one in which we're advertising?" We make the mistake of replying:

"I was concerned about this, too. So I looked up the circulation figures of both magazines and then I analyzed the readerships of the two magazines. The magazine we've been using has a bigger circulation but the readership of the other magazine is much more the kind of people who influence the buying decisions for our product."

Instead of answering the other person's question about how the specific circulations of the two magazines compare, we started by answering the different question, "How did you find out about the circulation of the two magazines?" The other person never asked this question, and while he may have liked the answer, he certainly didn't want to hear it first. He is trying to decide where he will get the most for his advertising dollar, and he can't make this decision from what we've told him. We haven't quantified, and without quantification he can't decide.

Here again, considerateness is pragmatic. Responding to our needs rather than to his, we defeat ourselves. He is likely to infer that we are deliberately withholding the quantification. Perhaps we don't have it; if not, why don't we say so and promise to get it? He may conclude that the quantification is not in our favor. And since we are willing to propose an action without having a clear case for it, our credibility suffers.

Beginning the Feed-In Remark

When the other person asks for information, and that information goes against our position, our anxiety may cause us to overexplain before providing the facts. But a lengthy explanation suggests that we are concerned more with winning our case than with arriving at the wisest decision. And when we substitute explanations for answers, we might unconsciously omit unfavorable information that we'd rather not give. If we do this, and are found out, our credibility diminishes.

When feeding in information, we're so absorbed in communicating the information itself that we often lose sight of what we're sending between the lines. But the sensitive listener is tuned in to emotions and motivations. When we play down unfavorable information, when we are evasive, or when we delay answering, we underestimate the other person's intelligence and lose our credibility much more easily than we realize.

The best answer is a direct answer; it is both easy to grasp and credible. If the other person asks a yes-or-no question, begin the answer with "yes," "no," or "I don't know." Suppose he asks, "When you estimated how much we'd save by buying this more expensive machine, did you figure the increased maintenance costs?" Answer with a "yes" or a "no"; don't start with, "Well, actually, the maintenance on this machine is not that much higher than on the machine we've been using." That does not answer his question; you can include that statement in your answer, but it should not begin your answer.

If the other person asks for a figure, begin the answer with that figure if you can. For example, if he asks, "How soon can you get me the information?" you should answer specifically, "Within a week." Don't start with, "This kind of information is difficult to get. I would have to check several sources."

Another useful device is to start the answer with wording similar to that of the question. Suppose the other person asks, "How will you get them to cooperate?" We begin our answer with the words, "I'll get them to cooperate by. . . ." In fact, the word "by" in itself is a good starting point for an answer to a question that asks how something will be done.

The beginning of the feed-in remark, or the *point* of the feed-in, should give the essence of the remark so that the other person is immediately oriented to the direction that the remark will take. The point of the feed-in remark in answer to a *why* question is the *because* that answers that question. If the other person asks, "Why don't we take Jim along on this trip?" you might respond, "Because he's needed here to complete a project that has to be finished by the end of this month." Any statement about why the project is more important than Jim's going on the trip should come only after the beginning statement that gives the essence of the answer.

The other person asks, "How will you finish this job in three days?" "By working overtime," is the answer that immediately tells him what action will be taken. Explanations of how much overtime, who will work overtime, or why overtime is the best way to do it may follow as elaboration.

Elaborating the Point
of the Feed-In Remark

In persuasion, our feed-in remarks implant in the other person's mind the premises that support his taking the action we suggest.

The other person's question is the invitation for us to implant a premise. To make our premise take hold, we have to go beyond the point of the feed-in remark and respond, as well, to the intent of the question. What does the other person really want to know? Answering his question requires us to elaborate, to substantiate, and often to give more than is explicitly requested. This part of the feed-in remark is the *elaboration.*

After the point of the feed-in remark, we may continue with elaboration if it will make our argument more clear or convincing. We might want to explain how we arrived at our answer, how it should be implemented, what the likely outcome will be, or what the significance of our answer is for the decision we want the other person to make.

The elaboration should be brief—roughly, under thirty seconds—but how long we talk should depend on the content. If the elaboration consists of figures and facts, it should be kept well under thirty seconds; if it is a narrative, it can run longer. We ought to imagine ourselves listening to our own elaboration and say no more than we, ourselves, could absorb well enough to explain it to another.

Forming the Question to Get Feedback

In responding to the other person, we must consider the questions: Did we interpret his question correctly? Did we answer the question he intended to ask? Was he listening? Did he interpret our answer as we meant it? By asking for feedback, we can learn whether he has absorbed the information, how he has interpreted it, and how he feels about it. Our seeking feedback also prods the other person to think about what we've told him.

The question part of the feed-in remark should not go beyond getting the other person's reaction to the information just fed in. (Don't ask the other person's reaction to the overall proposal unless you are ready to ask for a commitment.)

Suppose we propose that an important project be undertaken. The other person asks, "Where would you get the people for this project?" The point of the feed-in would be, "We would take them from our least important project." We then follow with the elaboration, "This would delay our least important project by three months, but we could afford to do this, considering the benefits it will bring."

Now, in our question for getting feedback, we want to ask only for a reaction, not for further reasoning. In this case, the question that concludes our feed-in remark might be, "Do you think we could take the people from our least important project, considering the benefits?"

If we are asked a question and are unsure of its intent, we should put some interpretation on the question and answer it. Then, by using a question, we should try to find out whether our answer was adequate. It is better not to answer a question with another question. Of course, if we do not understand what the other person means, we have to ask for clarification. Getting feedback is an essential part of implanting information in the other person's mind so that it becomes part of his reasoning in forming his conclusion.

The Midway Cue

While the other person's question or statement of agreement is a cue to us to feed in information to him, and his objection or statement of disagreement is a cue to us to draw out his underlying reasoning, there is another cue that falls midway between the two. This is the other person's objection, accompanied by his qualification that his perception of the situation may be wrong.

When the other person says, "You'll never get that job finished in two weeks," he is making a flat objection. But if he says, "I don't see how you're going to finish that job in two weeks," he indicates that he's not so sure you won't do it. He is more open to receiving information when he qualifies his objection by implying that his perception might be at fault.

This kind of cue, which falls midway between a feeding-in cue and a drawing-out cue, can be treated as either. What you do should be determined by the context. If you feel the other person lacks certain information, provide it. If you feel that he is placing a different weight on one or more of the premises, draw him out by exploring his doubts. "I don't see how" generally means "If I am to see how, I need more information."

"I don't see how" indicates that the other person hasn't been able to arrive at the same conclusion as we, but it doesn't imply that he has reached a different conclusion. The phrases "I don't think" and "It seems to me" indicate that the other person has arrived at a different conclusion. Often these phrases merely reflect caution, modesty, or conservatism—as though omitting them when giving an opinion would be too aggressive.

When the other person's remark contains both a question and an objection, we should treat it as a cue for a feed-in. His question indicates some degree of openness, and we should take advantage of this since we are trying to implant our premises. In the elaboration we can address the objection as well. But the feed-in should be primarily addressed to the question.

Suppose the other person says, "How would you expect anyone in this department to do that kind of a job? It's much too difficult and would take a lot of time."

Your feed-in might be, "By giving the person special training. This would take about three weeks but we'd save about $5,000 a year. While it is fairly difficult to do, Jim Parker has had some experience with this kind of operation and should be able to learn it. Would you consider it worthwhile to give Jim Parker the three weeks of training and make it part of his job, to save the $5,000 a year?"

Being Brief and Specific

When we feed in more information in a single remark than the other person can absorb, he's going to lose some of it; and what he loses may be crucial. Too often, when it's our turn to talk, we concentrate on getting the information out of us rather than into him. We try to bring out at one time all the information that will make our case instead of limiting our remark to what the other person can absorb.

As a rough guide, then, when describing or explaining we should keep each remark under thirty seconds, and we should ask the other person to comment after each remark. We should limit adjectives or figures to three in one remark. The best method is to feed in a little information at a time, get the other person to react, and then feed in a little more.

Be specific. Too often we talk in broad terms, referring to a place as having recreational facilities when we mean tennis courts and a swimming pool. Why speak of audio-visual equipment when we mean a sound slide projector? or mention "a musical instrument" when we can say "the clarinet"? or request more office equipment when we need another typewriter and a dictating machine?

When the other person hears the broad term, he has so many different specific concepts to choose from that he doesn't know quite what to picture in his mind. Our meaning is vague, and the ambiguity makes him uncomfortable. In order to have some definite picture in his mind, he may make an assumption; if he is wrong, there will be confusion. Moreover, if we use broad terms, we can create the impression that we are uncertain or confused.

When feeding in information, we need to listen with the other person's ears to what we are saying. Are we giving him the kind of information he wants? Are we enabling him to follow us immediately, giving him a quick overview or a direct answer, rather than keeping him waiting while we lead up to our point? Are we giving him an amount of information that he can readily hold on to, or are we flooding him with facts? Are we describing what's in our mind as we picture it so that he in turn can build a specific picture in his mind, or are we just giving him broad terms and vague generalizations? Let's feed in information as we would want information fed to us.

10 Coping with Each Other's Emotions

Drawing Out Emotions

If someone is emotionally excited at the very moment when we want him to see the sense of what we're saying, we have to delay our rational discussion to first help him talk out his pent-up feelings. For these distract him from reasoning. Just as our fingers stray toward a wound that is tender, to feel it all around, as though some understanding we might gain from touching it would help ease the pain, so our mind clings to an emotion, running over it, examining it, playing with it.

Trying to argue someone out of his feelings in order to eliminate the distraction doesn't work, because our arguments will be based on a combination of *our* observations of and *our* reactions to the circumstances. One's present reactions are determined partly by past experiences, and his are different from ours.

The explanation of a particular emotional reaction resides within the individual, but might not be available immediately even to him, let alone to another observer who has only the external facts. Someone may be angry or anxious or feel guilty without being aware of it; or he might be aware of it but at a loss to explain it; or what he thinks is the cause might be different from the real one. There might even be a number of causes all contributing to the same feeling.

For an individual to become aware that he is angry or anxious or guilty may require that someone else suggest this possibility to him. And for him to understand the cause of his feeling may require that someone else lead him on an exploration within himself.

When someone seems resentful or worried or guilty, your first move should be to sympathize with his feeling, to show your acceptance of it and to lead him in a comfortable way to become aware of it if he is not and to talk out his feeling. You should continue in this way as long as he continues to express emotion. Gradually, as the feelings are talked out he will become more reflective and less emotional, and you can move into a feeding-in and drawing-out to bring out both your reasoning and his.

Suppose a teenager complains:

"I hate Math. It's irrelevant. I have to waste all this time learning a lot of stuff I'll never use. It's boring."

The teenager is expressing feeling ("hate," "boring"), and you must respond to feeling first, before you get to the reasoning. You might say,

"It can be hateful to study something you think you'll never use."

You sympathized to show acceptance of the feeling, which encourages further expression.

"It really is. I spend a lot of time at it when I could be doing other things, and having fun, and I still get poor grades. It gets me. I'm getting A's and B's in all my other courses."

"It is upsetting to get poor grades after spending a lot of time, especially when you're doing well in your other courses."

You sympathized again since the teenager was still resentful ("It really is [hateful]," "It gets me").

"It's ruining my average. I put the same amount of time in on Math but I don't get the same grades."

The teenager seems to have subsided since he is only talking about what's happening rather than expressing feeling. You can now move to a draw-out remark to get at his reasoning.

"You do get better grades in the other courses, but why do you think you should get the same grade in Math just because you're putting in the same amount of time? Math may just be harder for you."

You acknowledged something true in his objection, drew out with a "why" question, and gave a reason for your question.

"It is harder. I've been studying but I do poorly on the tests. I don't know what to do."

In saying, "I don't know what to do," the teenager indicates openness since his "don't know" is equivalent to "tell me." Therefore, you can feed in.

"Perhaps you ought to spend more time on Math. Many people find some subjects easier than others. You could go for extra help and find out why you're falling down on the tests. Wouldn't it make sense to spend more time since you might find Math more difficult than other subjects?"

Your point of the feed-in gave him a direct answer, telling him what to do. Your elaboration supported and further explained your direct answer. And you followed with a question to get his reaction to your feed-in, and your question repeated your answer and the essence of its support.

"I don't have the time. I have too many other things to do."

He is objecting so you have to draw out.

"There are many things for you to do. How much extra time do you think you would need to get a good grasp of Math? Maybe it's less than you were thinking, and would be worth it."

Here, after acknowledging, you drew out with a "how much" question, and followed with the reasoning behind your question.

"I'd have to spend an hour at extra help twice a week. That's two hours I wouldn't have for something else."

Since he is still resisting, has not indicated openness, you have to continue to draw out.

"You would have to give up two hours' worth of something else a week. Is there something you're doing now that's worth less to you than getting an A or B in Math? You could give that up and come out ahead."

Here, you first acknowledged, then drew out with a "how much" question, since you asked for a comparison of quantities, and then gave your reason for the question.

"I guess I could give up playing ball a couple of times a week. I play enough ball, anyway, other days and weekends. I'd rather get good grades in Math."
"Fine. Give it a try. Once you catch up, you might not even need extra time."

Trying to reason with the other person about his emotion not only misses the mark because neither he nor we understand the various causes of his emotion, but it also frustrates the other person, who only wants to talk in order to relieve his excitement. It is kinder and more productive to listen to him and to encourage him, by sympathizing and by asking questions, to talk out his emotion. As he talks he will discharge his pent-up feelings and might see other causes of his emotion that he was unaware of. He may also come to wonder why he is so angry or so worried about such a thing.

The usefulness of getting the other person to talk out his disturbing feelings in order to eliminate them was illustrated in an experiment in which two groups of people were made angry by derogatory remarks about them, but only one group was allowed to communicate hostility toward the person who had made them angry. The people who were allowed to communicate their hostility to the person who had aroused it subsequently made fewer hostile comments and more friendly comments to that person than did the people who were not given a chance to communicate their feelings.[1]

Someone tells us he is worried about a test he has to take. Rather than give him advice or reassurance, we would do better to tell him we're sorry he feels upset and ask him what specifically bothers him about the test. As he talks, his anxiety is likely to subside.

If we're twenty minutes late in meeting someone, we should follow our apologies with a sympathetic question such as, "Have you been waiting long?" This will give him an opportunity to let out more anger.

When someone is pleasurably excited in telling us what a great athlete his son is, we only frustrate him by responding with stories about our own son's gifts. Instead, asking him what sports his son is particularly good at will give him a chance to release more of his joyful feelings. Feelings press for discharge and we respond to this pressure by letting out the emotion through our remarks. Yet we don't realize at the time that our need to discharge feeling is behind our talking. In an old comic routine, the straight man, observing wild excitement in the comic, asks the comic why he's excited. The comic, in high-pitched vehement tones replies, "Who's excited? I'm not excited."

1. Thibaut, John W., and John Coules, "The Role of Communication in the Reduction of Interpersonal Hostility." *Journal of Abnormal and Social Psychology*, 1952, Vol. 47, pp. 770–777.

Various Ways of Expressing Feelings

People discharge their anger largely unwittingly, in a variety of ways: through excessive or destructive criticism; by over-arguing; by withholding requested information when there's no reason for withholding it. Similarly, people express anxiety when they ask for help in making a decision from someone who is less capable than they are of making that decision; when they keep remaking their decision after it's too late to change it; or when they hesitate to make a decision when that decision is obviously the one to make.

Our "unfelt" feelings can become a barrier to our breaking through to each other. When we're angry at someone, we may turn down a request of his because of our anger and at the same time rationalize our refusal to him. As we explain it to him, we even believe that our own logic is the basis for turning him down rather than our means of *justifying* it. When we're anxious about something, we tend to talk about it in a repetitive way, going over it again and again, as though we were trying to gain control of the situation so that the feared thing could not happen. And when we feel guilty about something, we tend to confess it, as though asking forgiveness, wanting the other person to approve and accept us in spite of what we've done. We're not fully conscious of anxiety or guilt; we just feel as though we want to talk it over.

Our anger can make us sarcastic, overly critical, unresponsive to the other person's comments and questions. Our anxiety might distract us from listening, cause us to talk too much, make us ask for commitments that can't yet be given. Our guilt might cause us to steer the conversation continually to what we feel guilty about, simply because we'd rather talk about that.

Our need to express anger conflicts with our need to feel rational. This conflict generally produces a compromise in which the attack is only partly justified by rationality; the angry conclusions are really not warranted by the premises, but there is at least a show of reasoning.

As we attack, realizing at the same time that we're angry, we often temper what we say. We see that perhaps we went too far, and we take back some of our conclusions or modify them. Rationality reasserts itself as anger subsides. And when one makes the other person aware of the particular emotion operating within him at the moment, he can gain control of it. He can then separate the feeling within him from the content of his remarks.

When the other person is angry, we don't really know whether he is aware of his anger unless he acknowledges it. If he doesn't, we should start our response by suggesting to him that he may be angry. This might cause him to look inwardly to see if he is angry, and if he does recognize anger there, he is likely to reexamine his reasoning to see if he is being rational.

This doesn't necessarily mean that the other person will always accept our suggestion that he is angry. He may deny it. But even if he denies it, he may begin to admit it to himself and look at his reasoning more objectively—gradually shifting his position as he feels comfortable doing so.

A supervisor asks a subordinate to perform a chore that is unpleasant, and the subordinate flares up:

"What, again! I'm getting sick and tired of your dumping all the lousy jobs on me. You got something against me? How come I'm on your little list? Give one of these jobs to some other guy for a change, and let me live too."

What the subordinate is saying may or may not be true—the supervisor may have been assigning him a disproportionate share of the unpleasant tasks without realizing it. On the other hand, the subordinate may be angry about something else and taking this opportunity to discharge his anger. In either case he is angry, and this anger must be dealt with first, by referring to it sympathetically both to make sure he is aware of it and by encouraging him to express it. A question may be added to further encourage expression. The supervisor does this:

"I can understand your being angry if you've been getting all the crap jobs. I don't think you've been getting more than your share of them, but I could be wrong. What's going on?"

Referring to the subordinate's anger, the supervisor alerts the subordinate to the possibility that he might be distorting the situation because of his anger. And by admitting that he could be wrong, the supervisor increases his credibility with the subordinate. Finally, the supervisor draws out the subordinate's anger by asking him a very general question in order to get him to talk some more.

Even if the subordinate denies his anger, his looking inward to see whether he is angry might make him admit it to himself. The subordinate replies:

"Hell, I did that lousy job last week and the week before. Don't tell me you're not picking on me. Okay, so maybe some of the other guys do it once in a while, but not that often."

Here the subordinate expresses more of his angry feeling, but he tempers it a little by acknowledging that the other fellows do the job once in a while. The concession indicates some subsiding of his anger and a move toward objectivity. Now the supervisor can move from a very general question designed to draw out anger, to a more specific question to get at the subordinate's reasoning, as in the draw-out process. However, since the subordinate still expresses some anger, acceptance of this anger should be included in the manager's acknowledgment part of his draw-out remark, along with recognition of any truth or plausibility in the subordinate's logic. He uses a "what if" question:

"It's true that you're doing it more often now, and I can understand your being irritated by it. But what if the need is much greater now so that everybody is doing this unpleasant task more often? We're speeding up because this whole job has been given top priority."

Here the supervisor acknowledges both the feeling and also what is true, asks a question, and follows it with a reason for the question. The subordinate replies:

"I didn't know that. You mean the other guys are getting it every week now, too?"

The subordinate has now been motivated to seek information. Realizing that he might have been wrong, he is now open to the supervisor's ideas.

Similarly, when someone is worried about something, perhaps about a presentation he has to make, he may talk anxiously about it, wondering whether he'll be able to convince the audience. He might complain that some of the people are hostile and would like to prove him wrong. Rather than try to reassure him that he knows his material and will be impressive, we ought to make him aware that he is anxious and give him a chance to relieve his anxiety. We might say something like, "You seem worried. What specifically is bothering you?"

We need to become more conscious of emotional reactions, to respond to them by drawing the other person's attention to them and encouraging him to discharge them. We must hold back on our reasoning until we see some indication that the emotion has been resolved.

A man is angry because the cleaner has failed to deliver his suit on time. Keyed up by his anger, the man wants to vent it, to talk it out and get rid of its discomfort. His anger moves him to attack the cleaner:

"That damned cleaner. He's all screwed up. I told him I needed the suit by today and he said, 'Oh, sure, we'll have it for you,' and then he doesn't do a thing about it. You can't depend on them. They just don't give a damn, and here I've been using them for years."

In his need for release he has become irrational, abandoning the facts and imagining conditions to justify his attack. If the cleaner really didn't give a damn and was truly undependable, the man would have stopped using him long ago. The man is ignoring a history of on-time deliveries and overlooking the possibility that the delay might have been the result of unavoidable circumstances. The man has not thought to get the facts.

At the moment, he really doesn't want the facts. What he wants is to attack because he is angry.

If we fail to understand this, we can make the mistake of trying to reason with him:

"They've given you good service all these years. Something unavoidable must have happened this time. I'm sure they must have wanted to deliver it on time."

Here we are trying to eliminate his anger by dislodging the premises on which he seems to be basing it. But this is likely to make him even angrier as it blocks him from something else he wants—to attack. Instead, we need to sympathize with his feeling to encourage him to talk it out:

"I know how you feel. It can be damned annoying to count on a suit you really want to wear, and then not have it delivered on time."

If he is still angry and wants to attack some more, he can do so comfortably since we accepted his angry remark rather than try to refute it.

"You're darn right. It's my favorite suit and I wanted to look my best for this meeting. I told the cleaner it was important that I have the suit by today."

He's still angry ("You're darn right") so you sympathize to encourage his further expression of feeling. You can't get him to consider the reasoning until he subsides.

"It is disappointing not having the suit you want to wear."
"I suppose I have other suits that I like that I could wear. It's just that he said he would definitely have it."

He has subsided now and is open to reason. You can draw him out.

"Since he promised it, I can understand your annoyance at his not having it. How often has he disappointed you in the past? Perhaps something unexpected happened, a machine broke down or someone quit."

You first acknowledged the plausibility of his reaction, then drew out with a "how much" question, and followed with a reason for the question.

"He does give good service. Something must have happened. I don't know why I got so angry. I ought to roll with it better."

Expressing Anger by Characterizing

When the other person is angry at us, we still have to give him an opportunity to attack verbally in order to discharge his anger. This is much more difficult to do; his attack on us is likely to make us angry and want to attack in return, and that will only make him still angrier and even more inclined to attack—and a vicious circle ensues. His attack is likely to make us angry because he will probably hit us where he feels he can hurt us, in our self-image. Rather than rage about the specific thing we did that upset him, he will try to wound us with generalizations about our character. In our anger, we are likely to strike back by characterizing him negatively.

Therefore, we have to be careful not to tell people what they're like when we're annoyed at a specific act of theirs. Focus your criticism on the act. Don't characterize the person. If someone borrowed something from you and didn't return it, express your anger, if you wish, about the unreturned item, but don't call him irresponsible. It hurts him too much.

If you characterize negatively, which you're tempted to do when you're angry since you know such characterization is a potent weapon, the other person is likely to retaliate by doing the same. The successive escalation of attack and counterattack, in the guise of corrective comments, will not bring about any constructive changes in behavior, just bad feeling between you.

When we are criticized for having particular character traits, we need to remember that the criticism represents just one view; and that the other person's perceptions are partly determined by his own needs. Remembering this will help make the criticism less wounding. We can take what worth there is from it, and not need to defend ourselves.

Evaluate any criticism of your character for its validity. Don't accept it as necessarily true, nor reject it out of hand. What is the evidence that supports it? How does it compare with the observations of others?

To help you do this, keep in mind that even if we were to get the gift that the poet Robert Burns asked for all of us—to see ourselves as others see us—we would not see ourselves as we really are since each one of us sees the same person differently. Each brings his own past to his view so that each person's view is a mixture of what is and of how he feels about it. If we say very little, one person may see us as wise since we don't say foolish things, while another may consider us foolish because we don't say clever things. Some may think our quietness reflects kindness because we seldom criticize; others may think us hostile because we seldom praise. Some may think us selfish because we seldom give information; others may find us considerate because we listen so well. Seeing ourselves as another sees us is useful because it can make us question our own view of ourselves. But it doesn't tell us the truth about ourselves. We would approach this only by selecting from the observations of other people the things about us on which they agree.

A woman feels angry at her husband because he still hasn't fixed the stopped-up drain in the first floor bathroom sink. Once again she has to go upstairs to a second floor bathroom in order to use the sink. Suddenly, she erupts:

"I'm sick and tired of your promises to fix that sink. You don't care about me at all. You don't care if I drop from exhaustion. I have to climb up and down those stairs every time I want to use the bathroom sink. You're just not dependable. All you care about is your own comfort. If it was you that had to run up those stairs, that sink would be fixed in a moment. But why bother about me? I'm just a household drudge. You never think of anyone but yourself, and I'm sick and tired of it."

Irritations from many sources can very well be feeding into this woman's stream of anger at her husband's not having fixed the drain.

The woman's anger at her husband was too violent to have been caused by a stopped-up drain alone. If her husband really were inconsiderate, she could be letting out all the past frustrations she has suffered because of his selfishness. If he is normally kind to her, her anger may be swollen by other frustrations in her life.

She is not aware of the causes of her anger. It seems to her only that the stopped-up drain is the cause. Without questioning the magnitude of her passion, without considering the disproportion between her attack and the trouble that the drain has caused her, she lashes out. She requires just enough rationality so that she doesn't sound crazy; the stopped-up drain provides the semblance of reason.

In the same way, other streams of feeling from various sources flow together to form rivers of emotions such as anxiety, guilt, shame, jealousy, grief, regret, and even happiness. When we are worried or sad, we aren't usually aware of all the underlying contributors; we generally focus our feeling on one particular thing as the cause of it all.

She may be frustrated with the endless monotony of household chores; she might resent not having her own professional career and more household help; her daughter may have gone to a friend's house instead of helping her; perhaps her husband has been too busy to give her much attention in recent weeks; and maybe she's angry with herself for not holding to her diet enough to take off the ten pounds she wants to lose.

Some or all of these frustrations may have flowed together to make up the stream of anger that propelled her attack. Having had to climb the stairs again because of the stopped drain, she made her husband the target of her general anger. Wanting to hit hard and hurt bad, she attacked him at a particularly sensitive point: his feelings about his own character. Striking at the other person's character hits hard because it mobilizes his self-doubt.

Almost all of us have some doubts about ourselves, whether it be about our appearance, our intelligence, our kindness, our generosity, our consideratness, our drive to be productive, our likeableness, or whatever. To varying degrees, we feel we are what others say we are. We cherish compliments as reassurances that counteract self-doubts. We experience discomfort because of these doubts. When they are intense, they cause depression.

When a wife tells her husband that he is selfish, his anger wells up. But why is he made angry by words? This reaction is logical only if we really were made selfish—or however we're labeled—by what the other person says. The fear of a magic power in words to make things happen is seen in fairy tales where words can change people into frogs or swans or trees.

If the wife's characterization makes the husband feel selfish and undependable, he is likely to strike a blow at his tormentor by characterizing negatively in return:

"You're just plain spoiled, with a vicious temper. All you do is nag, nag, nag. Don't you think I've got other pressures on me? You damn well don't because all you think about is making life easy for yourself."

This would result in a raging response from his wife. However, suppose he recognized that he isn't necessarily what she says he is, and sympathizes instead:

"It is damned upsetting to have to run upstairs every time you want to use the sink, with all the other things you have to do. I didn't realize it was that bad."

"Damned right you didn't realize. You're caught up in your own little world and you don't know or care that I'm killing myself keeping things going. Just a little thoughtfulness and you could have gotten that drain repaired."

The husband is hurt again, and again tempted to hit back, but he controls the urge and continues to sympathize:

"I have been tied up lately and haven't given you and the house the attention I should. I know how frustrating that can be for you, especially when you're knocking yourself out with the other housework and the kids."

"Well, it's tiring going up an extra flight of stairs so many times, with all the running around I do. And you did promise to fix it three weeks ago."

She's subsiding now and is probably open to a little reason if it's combined with sympathy.

"Yes, I did, and my letting you down on that must be darned annoying. Look, I'll definitely work on it tomorrow night. Can you hold out till then?"

"I guess I can. I know you've been under a lot of pressure lately. A lot of things are eating at me and they must have triggered off my temper. But do it tomorrow."

We don't look enough in the direction of our feelings, and, consequently, we are too often unaware of them. It would be helpful for you to monitor the conversation continually both for your own expressions of feeling and for those of the other person, to see if either of you is being pushed away from thinking together. This will help both of you to stay on track, both by giving you greater control over your own expression of feelings, and by enabling you to guide the other person by sympathizing to make him aware of his feelings, and to encourage him to express them.

11 Case 1: Manager
Persuading Subordinate

In this chapter, and in the next four chapters, we will present a variety of situations that illustrate the application of the theories and techniques of persuasion that we have been discussing.

A manager who has five supervisors reporting to him has called in one of them to discuss the difficulties this supervisor has been having with the eight people who work under him. Four people who had worked for this supervisor have quit, and three of these four attributed their quitting to problems of getting along with him.

Of the eight people now working for this supervisor, two have complained to the manager about the supervisor's lack of communication with them. They say that the supervisor criticizes generally but avoids going into specifics, that he neither praises his workers nor shows them how to improve their performance. He is impatient with them, does not explain their duties fully enough, never asks for their opinions, and offers few of his own.

We begin with examples of two opening remarks that the manager should *not* make. The subsequent remarks will correctly apply the persuasive communication system described in earlier chapters.

Manager: Tom, communication is a vital part of your job. Through your communication with your subordinates you educate them to the duties of their job and guide them toward doing still better. You let them know when they're doing well and when they're doing poorly. This gives them satisfaction in their work because they feel that they're growing in the job by learning more and that they're appreciated when you praise them. They want to communicate with you just as you want to communicate with me. Too often communication gets neglected. We've got to keep the lines open.

Here the manager is slowly leading up to his point while the supervisor wonders, What's he getting at? Why is he telling me this? The supervisor, trying to extract meaning from the information fed to him, is likely to jump to the wrong conclusion about the boss's intention. To prevent this, the boss should have begun by saying what he wanted and what would have been gained by it.

Here is another possible way of opening the conversation:

Manager: Tom, what do you think of the way you communicate with your subordinates?

In opening with a question, the manager has done two things that work against him: he has begun by asking for rather than giving something, and he has made his question ambiguous by not indicating specifically why he asks the question. The reason for the question really defines the question. When the supervisor is confronted with this ambiguity, he is likely to become anxious and wary about committing himself to an answer.

To give information rather than to ask for it would allow the other person to relax and to feel his way into the situation. But this must be done without leading up so that the other person can see the point immediately.

Manager: Tom, if you were to communicate more with your people, we could save $45,000 a year in agency fees and training. That is what it cost to replace the three people who left your department because of difficulties in communicating with you. What do you think of the idea of your communicating more fully with your people if it would result in saving $45,000 a year in employee turnover expense?

Here the manager started with his suggested action (communicate more fully) and followed with his quantified end benefit (save $45,000 a year). The immediate benefit (reduced employee turnover) explains where the end benefit of $45,000 a year comes from. The question that concludes the proposal repeats the suggested action and the end benefit.

Supervisor: I'm a hell of a good communicator, but those three characters would've talked my ear off. They were always at me. I wouldn't have gotten anything done if I didn't cut them off. I'm damned well rid of them.

Since the supervisor is expressing anger, the manager has to sympathize to encourage expression of feeling:

Manager: I know how annoying it can be to have people interrupt you with their problems when you're trying to get other work done.

Supervisor: Communicating is important and I try to do it, but those three people who blamed their leaving on me wanted to talk over every little thing. If I did that much communicating I wouldn't have time for anything else. I want the kind of people who can work on their own and figure things out for themselves.

The supervisor's angry excitement has subsided so the manager can focus on the reasoning. The supervisor is objecting. An objection is a cue for the manager to draw out the reasoning that underlies the objection. The supervisor's premises are: the three people who quit wanted to talk about every little thing ("every little thing" remains unspecified) and talking about every little thing takes up too much time. His conclusion is that he would not get anything else done if he were to communicate as much as they wanted.

The manager should try to find out what the supervisor means by "every little thing." (When we encounter adjectives we should ask the other person to quantify or to become specific.) However, first he should acknowledge something true, possibly true, or plausible in the supervisor's remark. And then, after asking his question, he should follow by explaining why he is asking the question.

Manager: I can understand your feeling that there's a limit to the number of things you can talk about with your people and that they ought to be able to handle some of these things by themselves. Could you give me some examples of the kinds of things they wanted to talk about that you felt were not worth discussing? The reason I ask is that we ourselves know so much about these jobs we supervise, we sometimes take for granted a worker's knowledge and underestimate his need for guidance.

Supervisor: Well, take Joe, for example. He was always coming up with ideas that he wanted to talk over. Once he wanted to put a drinking fountain in our department so that everybody wouldn't waste so much time walking down the hall for a drink of water. When I pointed out we didn't have the plumbing connections here, he suggested we get a water cooler with bottles of water. I told him it was our policy to use only drinking fountains because we didn't want to get involved with bottle deliveries and bottle storage and breakage of bottles, and he said he could see the point, but there was a lot of time being wasted walking down the hall and stopping to talk to other people on the way to getting a drink. I can't be going into all these things for every idea someone brings up.

The supervisor is still objecting. He answered the manager's question by elaborating on his objection and giving an example, but he is still in disagreement. He has not given a cue for the manager to feed in, so the manager has to continue to draw out the supervisor's underlying thinking.

Manager: It's true, we certainly can't go out and buy a water cooler and bottles of water ourselves, not when this is covered by company regulations that apply to all departments. But do you think the idea makes sense, generally, to save time wasted in walking for water and stopping for conversation? I was wondering if some of Joe's ideas might have value if they were modified.

Supervisor: Oh, sure, the idea makes sense. I wish we could do something about it. Every time someone goes off for a drink of water, ten minutes goes by before I see his face again. But we'd never get one anyway, because as soon as we did, everyone else would want one. So there's no point in talking about it.

As long as the supervisor continues to object, the manager has to continue to draw out the supervisor's underlying thinking. Doing so, the manager must maintain an open mind and convey this open-minded attitude to the supervisor by indicating that the supervisor might be right or wrong and that the manager only wants to find out the true picture by uncovering the facts.

Manager: Can you give me any other examples so that I can get a clearer picture of how Joe takes up your time in discussion?

Supervisor: Well, just the other day he came in and started talking to me about how Bill and Larry should be separated because they're always squabbling with each other. He said they seemed to rub each other the wrong way, that they're always digging at each other and getting each other mad, and it bothers everybody around them. Bill and Larry never told me anything about their problems, and nobody else ever complained either. I asked a few questions and found out that it's true—they are always at each other. I'm going to have a little talk with them and tell them they'd better act like grown men, and get along with each other, and stop making each other mad all the time. We can't keep shifting people around to different locations just to make sure they get along well with the guy next to them.

The supervisor's remark contains these premises: the two men frequently fight with each other; the supervisor can't keep transferring people until everyone gets along well with the person working next to him; the supervisor's having a talk with these two people will cause them to get along. His conclusion, which is implicit, is that Joe's idea is impractical and talking about it is wasted time.

If the manager disagrees with the supervisor's conclusion, he has to draw out the supervisor further by acknowledging his agreement with a premise that seems right to him, questioning a premise that he disagrees with, and giving his own opposing premise as a reason for his question.

Manager: I realize that you can't move people around to please everyone, but in this particular case do you really think that just having a talk with them will get them to alter their behavior toward each other? It seems to me that people don't change that easily.

The manager acknowledged that the supervisor can't shift people around to please everyone and then questioned the premise that having a talk would produce a change in the two men. He then gave his reason for the question, that people don't change that easily.

Supervisor: I see what you mean. I guess a talk wouldn't really do it. It might calm them down for a day or two but then they'd be at each other again. I guess I'll have to separate them.

The supervisor is now in agreement on the need for separating the two men. However, he hasn't yet agreed that discussions with his worker, Joe, are not wasting his time. The manager now looks for a commitment on this.

Manager: While Joe might sometimes bring up ideas that take up your time unnecessarily, don't you feel that this particular idea of his, to separate the two men, was worth discussing? I'm asking this to see if we can get a clearer picture of what communicating with Joe and others could mean for you.

The manager first acknowledged something plausible in the supervisor's position, then raised a question about an earlier premise of the supervisor's, and then explained why he was asking.

Supervisor: Yes, I guess Joe did have a good idea here. I should have talked about it some more with him, but I was so used to his other ideas not making sense that I guess I didn't listen hard enough to this one.

While the supervisor concedes that this idea of Joe's made sense, he still clings to the notion that none of Joe's other ideas were worth discussing. Yet the supervisor does not give any evidence to support this notion.

Manager: It may be true that some of his other ideas weren't worth discussing. However, how can you know this since you thought this idea wasn't worth discussing until we explored it together? Perhaps if you had listened harder to some of his other ideas, you might have found them worthwhile.

The manager first acknowledged something plausible on a conditional basis, saying "It may be true that" but not saying that it was true. Then he raised a question about the supervisor's premise that Joe's other ideas weren't worth discussing. Finally, the manager explained why he was asking.

Supervisor: Well, I guess I really can't be sure about all his ideas. Some of his ideas I was sure about because they had been covered before. But maybe if I had talked more about his ideas with him, I might have found some of them useful.

Manager: I'm glad that you've come to see communicating with Joe in a different light. Now what happened with Marge?

The manager wants to find out the supervisor's underlying thinking about communicating with the two other people who quit.

Supervisor: Marge was a different story altogether. She never had any good ideas to contribute. She did her job well but she was always coming in to tell me, in one way or another, what a good job she was doing. Here I am concentrating on developing a plan or a schedule or some new idea, and in she comes, interrupting me to tell me about something she was working on and how clever or quick she was in doing it. It took a while for me to get my mind focused again after she left. I'd have to cut her off quickly or she'd go on and on.

The supervisor's premises are: Marge visited the supervisor too frequently (frequency unquantified); her purpose in visiting him was to tell him how well she was doing her job; her doing this served no useful purpose, interrupted his train of thought, and wasted his time. His conclusion is that he had to cut her off to minimize the wasting of his time.

The manager now draws out the supervisor, first acknowledging the premise he can accept, then questioning one of the other premises, and then giving a reason for his question.

Manager: I know how annoying it is to be interrupted when you're concentrating, and I know that it takes time to get your mind back in the groove. What makes you think that she was coming in to tell you how well she was working? I just want to make sure that we're not overlooking some other possible reason.

Supervisor: Well, that's what she'd talk about. She'd tell me how quickly she finished a job, way ahead of time; or she'd talk about some way she worked out of doing something better; or maybe she'd tell me how well she was getting along with the other people. What other purpose could she have had?

The supervisor has given a cue for the manager to feed in information. By asking a question, he indicates that he is motivated to listen. The manager now forms his feed-in remark, the point of the feed-in, which is a direct answer, followed by elaboration on that direct answer. Then the manager asks a question to make sure that the supervisor has absorbed the feed-in information.

Manager: To get some comment from you about how well she was doing. Her real purpose might have been to get an appraisal from you so she could know whether or not she was doing well. Does this sound reasonable to you?

Supervisor: It could be, but people know how well they're doing, whether they're producing, whether they're getting along with others on the job. They know whether or not they're getting out the work.

The supervisor has returned to an objecting position. He is in disagreement with the manager at this point, and again the manager has to draw out the supervisor's underlying thinking.

Manager: It's true, we all have our own opinions about our own performance. But just to give you a different angle on this: are you satisfied with having only your own opinion of your performance, or do you want to have my opinion, as your boss, to see if it agrees with your opnion and to make sure that you're seeing it right?

The manager, in his draw-out remark, uses a role-reversal technique, putting the manager in Marge's position in order to give him a better perspective on what Marge wants.

Supervisor: Yes, I definitely would want to know what you think. I might think I'm doing well and be wrong. I'm beginning to see what you mean. I did the same with Larry. He was always asking questions about what to do. He was fairly new here, and I was always impatient with him. I never gave him full enough answers, or tried to find out what was really bothering him. I guess I do have to communicate more, but how am I going to find the time? I've still got to do the planning, the scheduling, the paperwork, and a million other things.

At this point, the supervisor is ready to listen. He agrees that he needs to communicate more, and he has asked a question, "Where will I find the time?" Both his asking the question and his expressing agreement are cues indicating that he is motivated to receive information. This calls for a feed-in remark from the manager.

Manager: By deciding beforehand that you will apportion a certain amount of your time to communicating with your subordinates. You ought to start by assigning a percentage of your time for all your communicating. Then subtract both the communicating you do upward to me and also what you do on the same level to other departments. The remainder is the percentage of communicating you will do with your subordinates. What do you think of apportioning beforehand time for communicating with subordinates to make sure you do it?

The manager's feed-in remark began with a direct answer, then elaborated, and finally asked a question to get the supervisor's reaction.

Supervisor: That sounds like a good idea. What percentage of my time do you think I should spend communicating with my subordinates?

The supervisor asked a question, and that is another cue for the manager to feed in information.

Manager: About fifty percent of your time. Studies show that managers actually spend about eighty percent of their time communicating. Of course, this includes all letters, memos, reports, and meetings. I figure that you would need about thirty percent of your time for communicating to me, to people on your level, and to others who are not subordinates. That would leave you half your time to communicate with your own people. What do you think of this plan?

The manager answered directly, making the figure requested the point of his feed-in. He then elaborated and followed with a question to get the supervisor's reaction.

Supervisor: Half my time! I don't think I could spend half my time communicating with subordinates and still get my work done. That's a lot of time, and I've got a lot of other things to do.

The supervisor is again objecting. This means that the manager cannot feed in more information; he must instead draw out the supervisor's underlying thinking.

Manager: It's true that you have a lot to do, but why do you feel that you can't do these other parts of your job in twenty hours, which is the fifty percent of your time left after you've spent fifty percent communicating with your subordinates? The reason I ask is that other supervisors seem to be doing it—there are no complaints about their communicating with their people.

After acknowledging, the manager draws out with a "why" question and follows with a reason for his question. As reason for the question, the manager gives opposing evidence (other supervisors seem to be doing it), and this tells why he wants to know how the supervisor arrived at his conclusion.

Supervisor: Well, I don't know what the other supervisors do, but maybe they don't do as good a job on their reports as I do. Maybe they don't put the same kind of effort into their planning and scheduling. You know I'm always getting special jobs in here and having to rearrange things to fit these special jobs in. I try to work it out carefully so that the regular jobs go on with as little disruption as possible. It takes time to think that through. Maybe the other supervisors aren't as thorough about these things as I am.

The supervisor is still objecting, and the manager must continue to draw out the supervisor's underlying thinking. Using a form of the hypothetical ("what if") question, the manager suggests a new premise. If the supervisor accepts this new premise, perhaps it will change his conclusion that he can't spend half his time communicating with subordinates.

Manager: Yes, you do write excellent reports and you do do a thorough job of planning. Let's consider another possibility. Do you think that you might actually be spending too much time on report writing and planning, trying to make it perfect, polishing and re-polishing your writing, and mulling over your decisions too much, to the point where it isn't worth the extra effort for the slight additional gain you might get? What I'm thinking is that your wanting to make your reports and your planning perfect might be making you impatient in your communications with subordinates.

The manager starts his remark with an acknowledgment of something true in what the supervisor has said, and then he introduces his new premise with a hypothetical question. He gives his reason for his question by explaining what he has in mind.

Supervisor: I don't know. I hadn't thought about it. I suppose it's possible. I am pretty careful and thorough and maybe a perfectionist, so perhaps I am overdoing these reports and other things. It does slow me down a bit, but what can I do about it? That's the way I am.

The manager's drawing-out of the supervisor has brought the supervisor to want to know something from the manager. In his next remark, the manager feeds in information, starting with a direct answer, elaborating, and then asking a question to get a reaction from the supervisor.

Manager: You can try setting a time limit on each task before you start it. You don't have to limit yourself absolutely to that amount of time, but you can use it as a guide. Try to stick within the time limit. Ask yourself before each step you take whether that step is really necessary. Maybe you're wasting time by going over it again and again. Do this for every task you undertake, whether you're at work or at home. After doing this for a while, you might change your habit, or at least arrive at a compromise between overdoing it and doing just enough. Do you think setting time limits is worth a try?

Supervisor: Yes, I guess it is. Anything that will help me work better, and even live better, is worth a try. But it isn't just perfectionism. My people keep coming in to talk to me, and they interrupt me. Every time I get an interruption it takes time to refocus my thinking, to get back my concentration. You know, when I think about it, my workers are really the ones stopping me from communicating with them. The more they interrupt me, the longer it takes me to do my thinking and the less time I have for communicating with them.

While the supervisor agrees to try setting time limits and to consider whether each step is necessary, he raises another point that the manager might question, that the workers' interruptions are partly responsible for the supervisor's not being able to communicate with them as much as he should. If the manager disagrees with this conclusion, he has to draw out the supervisor's underlying thinking. The manager starts with an acknowledgment, follows with a hypothetical question, and concludes with a reason for his question.

Manager: Well, that's one way of looking at it. What about the possibility that because you're not communicating with them enough, they're coming in and interrupting you in order to get the information they need? What I'm thinking is that maybe you could stop this vicious circle by communicating more fully with them so that they don't have to come in and interrupt you. Then you won't be using up so much time trying to recapture your concentration, and you can communicate more with them.

Supervisor: Well, I never looked at it that way. You're saying that I might actually be the one who's causing them to come in and interrupt me. But even if it were true, there's not much I can do about it because it gets down to the amount of time that's available. Just as I have a tendency to work things over too much, they have a tendency to want to talk too much. If I allowed them to do all the communicating they want, they'd use up all my time.

The supervisor is still objecting, which is a cue to the manager to draw out. The supervisor's reasoning goes like this: if no limits were placed on the subordinates' communicating, they would use up all my time; if my time were used up, I couldn't accomplish my job; therefore, I can't allow my subordinates to decide for themselves how much time they may spend communicating with me.

In order to acknowledge something plausible in the supervisor's objection, the manager can agree on a conditional basis. (We can always agree that if a premise were true, then the other person's conclusion would follow—without agreeing that the premise is true.) After his acknowledgment, the manager questions the premise and then gives a reason for his question.

Manager: If your subordinates continued to communicate as long as you allowed them to, I agree that you would never get your job done. But what makes you think that they'd continue to communicate until you stopped them? Perhaps because of your impatience you're somehow only expecting it to happen.

Supervisor: I have to admit I don't really know. It just seems that way from the way they talk. Maybe that's just my impatience. Maybe they would interrupt less if I communicated more. I wonder what else I could do to cut down on the interruptions. They really get me.

Asking what amounts to a question ("I wonder what I could do"), the supervisor is now open for feed-in from the manager. In his next remark the manager again answers directly, elaborates, and then asks a question.

Manager: You could try setting aside certain hours each day for communicating with subordinates. Ask them to wait until those hours to talk to you about a problem unless it's urgent. What do you think of this plan?

Supervisor: I had thought of that, but I was afraid that if hours were set aside, they would use the time unnecessarily just because it was available to them. But, like you said, maybe it's just my impatience that's causing me to expect this.

Since the supervisor has come to agree with the manager, the manager can now summarize and ask for a commitment.

Manager: That's good thinking. Now how about giving the three things we've talked about a try: communicating more fully with your subordinates; setting aside time for them to communicate with you; and setting time limits on your own tasks in an effort to cut down your overworking of tasks because of perfectionism?

Supervisor: Right. I'll do that and let you know how it works out. Thanks for your help.

12 Case 2: Spouse Persuading Spouse

A. Wife Persuading Husband

A wife wants her husband to make decisions when their children come to him, instead of telling them to "ask your mother." This couple has three children: John, age 14; Susan, 11; and Jennifer, 9.

Wife: Bill, do you think I ought to make all the decisions about what the children can and cannot do?

The wife makes the mistake of starting with a question. It is difficult for the husband to answer because he doesn't know what's going on. Is she about to criticize him? Does she want to discuss an article on child care that she's just read? Does she want to talk about how the neighbors rear their children? Ambiguity arises when our purpose is hidden.

It is better to begin by giving information rather than by asking for it. This eases the other person into the conversation. Consider another opening:

Wife: Jennifer came to me this morning and asked me whether she could go to the shopping center by herself. Since she was playing in the same room you were in, and I was upstairs, I asked her why she didn't ask you. She said she did, and you told her to ask me.

Here the wife makes the mistake of leading up to what she is getting at, which leaves her husband wondering what her point is going to be. There is a much better way to begin.

Wife: If you were to make decisions when the children came to you, instead of telling them to see me, you'd come across to them as more decisive and more caring. They would see that you were willing to take the time and effort to think a situation through and to commit yourself to a decision about it. What would you think of making the children feel that you were decisive and responsible and caring by making decisions about whether they can do something when they come to you about it?

This opening remark immediately gives the husband an overview. It contains the suggested action of making decisions, the end benefit of being more decisive and caring in the eyes of the children, the immediate benefit of showing that he is willing to take the time and effort to think through the decisions, and a question that repeats the suggested action and the end benefit. (In this case, the wife put the end benefit before the suggested action; it can come either before or after.) The end benefit was quantified only to the extent that the impression of decisiveness and caring would be greater than it is now, but this amount of quantification is all that is necessary, since any increase would make the suggested action worthwhile.

Husband: What do you mean? When did I send them to you for a decision?

The husband's questions are a cue for a feed-in remark. The wife can answer either question, but she should answer only one at a time, asking her own question to get her husband's reaction to her answer. Depending upon the husband's response, it may not be necessary for her to answer the other question. Generally it's better to answer the last question first; the other person, asking several questions at once, is usually working his way up to what he really wants to know.

Wife: You've done it whenever we don't have a clear-cut rule covering the situation. For example, just this morning, when Jennifer asked you if she could go to the shopping center by herself, you sent her upstairs to ask me about it, shifting the responsibility for the decision to me. Do you think that you tend to do this?

The wife starts by answering her husband's second question, "When did I do this?" Her response probably answers his first one ("What do you mean?") as well. Her remark began (the point of her feed-in) with a direct answer to his question, telling when he did it; then she elaborated by giving an example; finally, she asked a question to get his reaction.

Husband: I sent her to you because I thought you might need her around the house and I didn't want her to leave without checking with you.

The husband is disagreeing. By adding what the husband is saying to what he is implying we can reconstruct his reasoning: if Jennifer had gone to the shopping center, she wouldn't have been available for another activity here; although I had nothing in mind for her to do, her mother might have had; therefore, I sent her to her mother in case she wanted her here.

Another premise, unspoken but implicit is: it is all right for Jennifer to go to the shopping center alone. If it were not all right, the question of her availability for another purpose would not have been relevant. The wife doesn't agree that it's all right for Jennifer to go to the shopping center alone. Thus her husband's implicit premise is the one she needs to question when she draws him out.

Wife: I appreciate your thinking about her being needed for something else, but why do you think she should be allowed to go to the shopping center by herself? She has to cross several very busy streets, and that parking lot is dangerous—cars come from every direction.

The wife began her draw-out remark with an acknowledgment, then asked a "why" question. She gave her reason for the question when she referred to the busy streets and the dangerous parking lot.

Husband: I didn't say that I thought she should be allowed to go. I only said that you might have needed her for something else.

The husband disagrees with his wife's conclusion that he thinks Jennifer should be allowed to go. His disagreement is a cue for her to draw out his underlying thinking.

The husband explicitly stated these premises: I did not say that Jennifer should be allowed to go; I did say that I didn't know if you needed her for some other reason. Another premise implied in what he said is: whether or not I feel she should be allowed to go, it was relevant to find out if you needed her. This is the doubtful premise that the wife should question in her draw-out remark.

Wife: It's true that you didn't know whether I needed her, but why would this matter unless you felt she should be allowed to go? If you wouldn't allow her to go, she would still be here.

The wife acknowledged something true in her husband's objection. Then she raised a question and gave a reason for asking it.

Husband: I see what you mean. I guess it did sound as if I thought she should be allowed to go. But I don't think she should. It seems too dangerous to me.

The husband has been moved in his thinking to the extent of agreeing that he did imply that Jennifer should be allowed to go, although he doesn't feel this way now. However, he has not expressed agreement with his wife's earlier suggestion that he had sent Jennifer to her for a decision, and his wife has to continue drawing him out.

Wife: Yes, it is quite dangerous. Why didn't you tell her this? I'm wondering if perhaps you hadn't decided this when she asked you, but have just decided it now.

The wife starts by acknowledging something that she agrees with in her husband's remark. Then she draws him out to test her own thinking and to get her husband to face his. She asks for his reasoning and at the same time tells him what she has in mind.

Husband: Look, I don't know what the hell you want from me. I was tired and trying to relax. I didn't want to think about it. So I sent her to you. I don't think that's any great crime.

The husband is expressing irritation so the wife has to interrupt the reasoning to respond to feeling:

Wife: It's irritating to be interrupted when you're trying to relax.
Husband: It is. I just didn't feel like handling Jennifer's problems.
Wife: Making decisions is no way to relax when you're tired.

The husband has calmed down so the wife can return to reasoning.

Husband: Actually, I hadn't thought about it until just now. I guess when she asked me, I was absorbed in reading the paper, and maybe I didn't want to think about it at the moment, so I sent her along to you.

The husband admits, by implication, that he sent Jennifer to her mother not to find out whether she was needed, but to avoid making a decision. While he has come some distance, he still hasn't given any indication that he agrees that he generally sends the children to his wife for decisions. His wife has to continue to draw him out.

Wife: I can understand your being absorbed in the paper and not wanting to be distracted, but how often do you think you send the children to me for decisions? It seems to me, looking back, that it's often enough to show a pattern.

In her draw-out remark, the wife first acknowledged something plausible in what her husband said, then asked a "how much" question, and concluded with a reason for her question. Her acknowledgment and the reason for her question, both inputs of information, help rapport in two ways: they provide a giving (of information) both before and after a taking (a question is a taking of information); and they tell her husband that his ideas are being considered.

Husband: I don't think I do it hardly at all. At least, I'm not aware of it. Do you really think I do it that often?

The husband starts out with an objection and moves to a greater state of openness, admitting that he isn't aware. Finally, his question shows that he is open to receiving information. When both an objection (a cue for drawing out) and a question (a cue for feeding in) occur in the same remark, the cue for feeding in should take priority; feeding in is essentially what we want to do in order to build our case in the other person's mind.

Wife: Yes, I do. Do you remember last week when John came to you and asked if he could take guitar lessons? You told him to talk to me about it. Wasn't this sending him to me to make the decision?

The wife starts her feed-in remark with a direct answer to the husband's yes-or-no question, then she elaborates with her example in the form of a question. Normally, a question should not be used in the elaboration. However, her question is a rhetorical question—one not calling for an answer. She ends with another question to get feedback, hoping to stimulate her husband to think about what she has said and to commit himself on it.

Husband: Okay, I did send him to you that time. But Wednesday night Susan came to me to ask if she could sleep at a friend's house, and I told her she couldn't because she had school the next day and because we only allow the kids to sleep at a friend's house on the weekend. I didn't send her to you. I made the decision.

The husband's remark is an objection, and the wife has to draw out his underlying thinking.

Wife: It's true that you didn't send Susan to me for that decision, but did you really make the decision? We decided some time ago that the kids could have sleepover dates only·on weekends, and we set this rule with them then. It seems to me that you were just going by this rule rather than making a decision.

The wife started her draw-out remark with an acknowledgment of something true in the husband's objection. Then she asked a "why" question—her question is equivalent to "Why do you think you made a decision?"—and ended with a reason for her question.

Husband: Well, I guess I didn't really make a decision then, but I did participate in working out that rule with you. Therefore, I was a part of making that decision originally, wasn't I?

The husband is asking a question and a question is a cue for the wife to feed in. Her drawing out his thinking has brought him to a state of openness.

Wife: Yes, you were, definitely. I'm not saying that you never make decisions. But it seems to me that when the children come to you with requests, and the decisions require the situation to be thought through at that moment, you send them to me. Don't you think this is generally the case?

The wife started her feed-in remark with a direct answer to her husband's question. Her point of the feed-in was "Yes, you were, definitely." Then she gave her elaboration and asked a question to get his reaction.

Husband: Well, maybe I do send the kids to you for decisions most of the time. But you're with them so much more. You're much closer to these everyday situations. You have more of a basis to figure out what to do, just as I'm in a better position to make decisions about my work.

The husband again raises an objection, which is a cue to his wife to draw out the underlying reasoning that supports it.

Wife: It's true that I do spend more time with the children than you do. But don't you think you could make a good enough decision, considering the amount of time you do spend with the children, your own experience as a child, and your general knowledge and judgment about what is safe and what works in the world?

The wife began her draw-out remark with an acknowledgment of something true in her husband's objection. Then she asked an equivalent of a "why do you think question." Her reason for the question followed.

Husband: Yes, I can make good decisions about the children, but since you're closer to the situation, spend more time with them, and get a chance to talk to other mothers about these kinds of situations, why shouldn't you make the decisions?

The husband's question is the cue for the wife to feed in.

Wife: Because of the effect that that would have on the children. They would get the feeling that their father is either unable to make decisions or doesn't care enough. Even if I did have an edge on you in making decisions because I spend more time with the children—which doesn't necessarily give me an edge because you might have better judgment than I—I think that their seeing you as decisive and caring is more important than making the best decision. Don't you think that the children's seeing you as decisive and caring is more important?

The wife begins with a direct answer to the husband's "why" question, using the word "because" to form a response in line with the question. The wife then gives her elaboration, and she ends with a question to get the husband's reaction.

Husband: Yes, I have to agree. It certainly is more important for me to relate to the children in a decisive, caring way. I guess I wasn't aware of what I was doing and what it meant. Okay, I'll make the decisions when the kids come to me.

The husband has finally come to agree with his wife's original proposal.

Wife: Fine. Sometimes it's hard, but it's worth it.

B. Husband Persuading Wife

This husband wants his wife to stop allowing the children to interrupt the conversations that the husband and wife have with each other. The husband opens correctly.

Husband: The children are going to become discourteous to others in conversation if you go on allowing them to interrupt our conversation whenever they want. They'll come to feel that what they have to say is more important than what anyone else is saying. What do you think about their becoming discourteous in conversation if you go on allowing them to interrupt whenever they please?

In his opening the husband began with the end benefit, forming it in negative terms, as an undesirable result. His suggested action, by implication, is that the wife not allow the interruptions. His immediate benefit, following his suggested action, is an explanation of how the negative end benefit would result in the children's coming to feel that anything they say is more important than what others say. He ended with a question that repeated his suggested action and end benefit.

Wife: Oh, come on, Bill. I can't keep them standing around until we finish a conversation. Suppose it's something they need to know right away?

The wife starts with an objection and ends with a question. The question, a cue for feeding in, should take priority. (We should take advantage of any opportunity to feed in.)

Husband: Then answer it right away. But if it's not urgent, the child should learn to wait until we're through. He should be taught to decide for himself whether his question is important enough to interrupt our conversation. Doesn't teaching him to wait make sense to you?

The husband gave a direct answer to the wife's question, elaborated, and then followed with his own question to get her reaction.

Wife: Does it really happen that often?

The wife's question is a cue for a feed-in.

Husband: Yes, it does. Just a few minutes ago, Susan interrupted our conversation to ask you if she could go to the movies with Debbie on Saturday. There was no urgency about her getting an answer to this. She wasn't on the phone with Debbie. Yet you turned away from our conversation to discuss it with her. It seems to me that kind of thing happens about half the time we're talking when the kids are around. Think about it; does it seem that frequent to you?

The husband gave a direct answer to the wife's question, elaborated, and then asked a question to get a reaction.

Wife: Tell me, are you really concerned about the effect on the children, or are you bringing this up because the interruptions irritate you?

The wife has again asked a question, giving another cue for the husband to feed in information.

Husband: Both. I feel it's bad for the children, and also it does irritate me to have my train of thought interrupted and to be cut off in what I'm saying. Doesn't my irritation add to the importance of stopping them from interrupting?

The husband's point of the feed-in was a direct answer to the wife's question. He elaborated, then ended with a question to get her reaction to the new information he fed in. Preventing his irritation at the interruptions is actually another end benefit, and the husband has taken the opportunity to introduce it here.

The wife had asked her question as though the two possible results, being bad for the children and irritating her husband, were mutually exclusive. The husband used his point of the feed-in to reject his wife's implication that it had to be one or the other, when he said "Both." (We have to guard against being sidetracked by the other person's unwarranted assumptions. If the husband had accepted his wife's premise that it had to be one or the other, and if he felt that he was irritated by the interruptions, he might have said, "I guess it does irritate me, but you've got to admit that it can be annoying." The wife might then have ended the discussion by saying, "Yes, it can be annoying, and I'm sorry that it has to happen, but we do have to put up with some annoying things for the sake of the children." And the point that the husband had wanted to make would have been lost.)

Wife: Well, yes, I don't want to irritate you or do anything bad for the children, but it's hard for them to wait. They can't seem to do it. If they want to say something, they'll just decide it's important enough and they'll interrupt.

Here the wife objects that the children can't wait. Her objection is a cue for the husband to draw out her underlying thinking.

Husband: I agree they're impatient, but why do you feel that they can't wait? They certainly wait to speak in the classroom until the teacher calls on them. They don't interrupt the teacher.

The husband started his draw-out remark with something true in the wife's objection. Then he drew out with a "why" question and explained why he was asking. His reason for the question was at the same time an input that contained contrary evidence.

Wife: You've got a point there. I guess they can wait. But as grownups, we're so much more capable of waiting.

You know how children are. They get excited, and they want to have their say. I don't think we should keep them waiting around, full of excitement, just so we can continue our conversation without interruption. After all, I don't do this when you're telling me something urgent. I feel that if we're just talking politics, or you're telling me about something that happened in the office, we can afford to wait a moment to let them speak.

The wife is raising an objection, and an objection is a cue for the husband to draw out the underlying reasoning that supports her objection. Her reasoning contains the implied premise that people automatically acquire the ability to wait without interrupting, rather than having to learn it through practice. This is the doubtful premise that needs to be drawn out.

Husband: I agree that adults can generally wait more easily than children. But do they automatically acquire this ability, or do they have to learn it by exercising discipline and actually waiting until someone else is finished talking? I think we both have seen adults who have never learned to wait, who constantly interrupt, who can't bear to put off what they want to say at the moment.

The husband starts his draw-out remark with an acknowledgment of something he feels is true in the wife's objection. Then he raises the equivalent of a "why" question, using the do-you-think form (which is the same as "why do you think?"). He ends with a reason for the question stated in the form of evidence to the contrary.

Wife: You're certainly right about people we know who constantly interrupt or never let you get a word in. I guess they never did learn, and I certainly wouldn't want the children to grow up like that. But how are we going to get them to wait instead of interrupting?

The wife's remark is a cue for her husband to feed in information, both because she agreed and because she asked a question.

Husband: By telling them, as a general rule, that they must not interrupt unless it can't wait, and then punishing them if they do. We can also praise them when they observe this rule. After doing it for a while, it will become a habit with them, just like any other rule of courtesy. Do you think that if we give them the rule, and praise them when they follow it, and punish them when they don't, that they'll learn not to interrupt?

The husband's point of the feed-in was a direct answer to the wife's question. It began with "by," a useful word that guides the forming of an answer so that it directly fits the question. He then followed with his elaboration, and he ended with a question to get her reaction to his answer.

Wife: That sounds reasonable. The only trouble is that the kids are going to rationalize that whatever they want to say can't wait.

The wife has raised an objection again, and the husband has to draw out the underlying reasoning that substantiates her objection.

Husband: I guess they could interrupt and then try to justify it with some rationalization, but why would they want to when they know they will be punished if they do?

The husband started his draw-out remark with an acknowledgment, then used a "why" question, and finished with a reason for the question.

Wife: Then they'd say we're being unfair because they thought it was urgent.

The wife is still objecting, and the husband has to continue to draw out her underlying thinking.

Husband: Yes, that could be. What if we explored their justification fully, really making them back it up? Then they'd learn both not to interrupt and not to try to deceive us.

The husband began his draw-out remark with an acknowledgment. Then he drew out with a hypothetical ("what if") question, which he used to introduce a new premise. We use a hypothetical question when we know the reasoning behind the other person's objection, and agree that it makes sense, but we want to change one of the other person's premises to see if the other person will change his opposing conclusion. The hypothetical question is an input of information as well as a draw-out.

After the hypothetical question, the husband gave his reason for the question when he explained why his new premise would make his idea work.

Wife: Yes, that might work. It's going to take a lot of patience, but I think it's worth a try.

Now that the wife has agreed to the husband's proposal, he can close with a suggestion about when and how they will explain the new rule to the children.

13 Case 3: Salesman
Persuading Prospect

A salesman wants a prospect to engage the salesman's firm to conduct a series of workshops in persuasion for the prospect's managers, salesmen, engineers, and other personnel who have to interact persuasively.

Salesman: Would you tell me about the kind of training you're giving your managers now?

This opening remark is wrong in three ways: it asks for information rather than gives it; it does not provide an overview of where the conversation is going; and it does not motivate the prospect to pursue the conversation. Here is another common type of opening that is better, but still needs improvement.

Salesman: Persuasion is a vital part of every business. When managers persuade, rather than just give orders, they gain greater cooperation from subordinates. Subordinates have to persuade their bosses if they want to get action on an idea. Salesmen have to persuade prospects. When people work together as a team they each have to persuade the other to look at a different solution to the problem. Now, to make your people more productive and cooperative, and happier in their jobs, their ability to communicate has to be upgraded. This means giving them training in the techniques of persuasion. Doesn't this make sense to you?

The salesman led up to his point. It would have been better if he had started by explaining what he was selling and its benefit. Otherwise the prospect might quickly assume, before hearing the entire remark, that the salesman wants to sell a survey of the company's communication, a book on communication, or a method of testing employees for persuasion ability. And if he doesn't want what he thinks is being presented, the prospect may simply tune out.

Even if the prospect suppresses his tendency to jump to conclusions, his uncertainty is likely to become an irritation. There is an even better way to begin.

Salesman: If you engage us to conduct workshops in persuasion tailored to your company, you will get a four hundred percent return on your investment if, as a result, the productivity of those attending the workshop is increased by as little as five percent—and the increase might very well be ten percent, twenty percent, or even more. Would you consider using our workshop if it meant a possible return of four hundred percent or more on your investment?

The salesman opened with a suggested action: have workshops conducted. He then gave a quantified end benefit: a return of four hundred percent on the investment. The immediate benefit, an increase in productivity, tells where the end benefit will come from. He then ended with a question that repeated the suggested action and the end benefit. In estimating productivity, the salesman chose a low end-figure to maintain credibility. He also pointed out that the return could be much greater.

When we quantify, even conditionally and only with estimates, the favorable cost–benefit balance can readily be seen. And a conservative estimate seems plausible and motivates the prospect to find out more.

Prospect: You guys keep coming in here with your wild claims about saving me money or stepping up my productivity. I get tired of listening to these dreams all of you cook up.

The salesman has to interrupt his reasoning to sympathize with the prospect's feeling:

Salesman: I guess it does get tiresome listening to salesmen's stories.

Prospect: Sometimes it does. Our own salesmen are out there now prodding their prospects and handing out the same kind of dreams. Where would we be without them. Anyway, how will this workshop increase people's productivity?

The prospect's feeling has subsided. His question is a cue for the salesman to feed in information.

Salesman: The people attending will develop greater skill in communicating accurately and persuasively while maintaining rapport. This will result in more good ideas being implemented, fewer errors, less time wasted in discussion, greater effort, more products sold, and lower turnover of employees. Can you see how developing skill in persuasive communication could produce these results?

The salesman started with a direct answer, then elaborated, and then followed with a question to get a reaction.

Prospect: We're not having any trouble communicating. I haven't had any complaints about it.

The salesman must now uncover the thinking that supports this statement. It goes like this: When communicating is not being done well, we get complaints; therefore, since we're getting no complaints, we're communicating well. As his acknowledgment, the salesman could agree that the prospect had not gotten complaints about communicating. He could then draw out the support for the questionable premise that if communicating weren't being done well, people would complain.

Salesman: I can understand your feeling that communication is good because no one has complained. But what if your people aren't aware that communicating could be done better? They may assume that their communication, with all its faults, is normal, and they wouldn't think to complain.

After an acknowledgment, the salesman used a hypothetical ("what if") question to introduce another premise to see if it would affect the prospect's conclusion. His reason for the question followed.

Prospect: If they didn't know communicating could be better, maybe they wouldn't complain about it, but they'd know that something was wrong if they weren't getting their ideas sold, or a lot of errors were being made, or sales were down, or any of the other things you mentioned that depend on their communicating.

The salesman has to keep working on the reasoning behind the prospect's objection.

Salesman: If their ideas weren't being sold, if morale were low and sales were down, it's true that they would be aware that something was wrong. But why would they necessarily blame it on their own lack of skill in communicating when they could just as well blame it on something else? It would be easier for them to blame others than to blame themselves.

The salesman first acknowledged agreement with the idea that the employees would know when something was wrong. Then he drew out the prospect's doubtful reasoning that if they knew something was wrong they would attribute it to their own inadequate communicating. The salesman concluded with a reason for his question: it would be easier for people to fault something else than to blame themselves.

Prospect: You have a good point there. But we're doing well. Our sales are up, our profits are up, and employee turnover is low.

The prospect's thinking has to be further drawn out because he is still objecting. In saying that the company is "doing well," the prospect is thinking in either–or terms: the company is either doing well or it is not. This polarity of thought, this tendency to think in black-and-white terms, is encouraged by our language, which uses adjectives to indicate the presence or absence of a particular condition. We say that something is one way or, its opposite, the other: strong or weak, durable or perishable, simple or complicated, expensive or inexpensive.

When we encounter someone doing this we have to lead him from either–or thinking to continuum thinking, where he will see attributes as existing on a continuous scale. Then we have to help him find the appropriate point on the scale.

Salesman: I'm glad that you're doing well, but wouldn't you want to do still better if you could?

The salesman starts with an acknowledgment and then poses a hypothetical question to introduce the idea of the continuum, which continues beyond doing well. The unstated reason for the question is obvious.

Prospect: Sure, we'd like to do still better. We'd like to do as well as we could. How's this training in persuasive communication going to help us do better?

The prospect's question is a cue for the salesman to feed in information.

Salesman: By increasing your productivity and your sales. Since your managers will communicate more clearly and persuasively, they will have more good ideas implemented, and fewer errors will be made. They will do a better job of motivating subordinates. Because your salesmen will be more persuasive, they will sell more. So wouldn't clearer, more persuasive communication on the part of your managers and salesmen result in increased productivity and sales?

The salesman answered the question with the word "by" which provides a direct answer to a how-will-something-be-done question. The salesman elaborated, then asked a question to get a reaction.

Prospect: Well, it sounds plausible. But how will this workshop make my people communicate better and be more persuasive?

More information should be fed in.

Salesman: By giving them skill in communicating and persuading. These techniques enable them to get the other person to think along with them point by point, mind to mind, and to work through to the same conclusion. Instead of arguing with each other, with neither of them listening because each is thinking of what he's going to say next, they'll each be thinking about what the other is saying, using two minds to achieve the same end. Don't you think giving them skill in persuasive communication could make a big difference?

Again, the salesman used the word "by" to respond to the prospect's how-will-something-be-done question. The salesman then elaborated, and he ended with a question to elicit a reaction.

Prospect: Yes, it sounds good. Could you explain more specifically what they would learn? I want to make sure that this is the kind of thing they need.

Case 3: Salesman Persuading Prospect 125

The prospect's question is a cue for the salesman to feed in. Because he has much to convey, the salesman feeds in one segment of information at a time, asking for a reaction to each segment before going on to the next.

Salesman: They would learn a number of specific techniques. They would learn how to motivate others to listen and how to accommodate for the other person's tendency to tune out. They would learn how to organize their remarks in order to come directly to the point. Did you ever have someone start telling you something, and you didn't know what he was driving at, so you started jumping ahead of him, trying to figure out what his point was?

Prospect: Yes, some people drive me crazy that way. I always wish they'd get to the point. They seem to feel that they have to build their case. Often I don't even know what they want until we're almost through talking.

Salesman: Yes, it happens all the time. Your people would also learn when they ought to be telling the other person something because he's ready to listen, and when they ought to be drawing out the other person's underlying thinking because he's not open to ideas. They learn how to determine what another person bases his objections on, and how to make him aware of it. When somebody objects by saying, for example, "Oh, that's too complicated," we tend to answer by replying, "It's not complicated at all, it's very simple." Yet we don't know what "too complicated" means. We make assumptions about someone's underlying thinking and then respond to our own assumptions. Aren't we really talking to ourselves when we do this?

Prospect: Yes, I see what you mean. What we need is to find out more about the other person's thinking instead of talking so much ourselves.

The prospect's agreement is the cue for the salesman to continue to feed in.

Salesman: That's right. Your people would learn how to present information to another person, answering his questions directly, so that the information takes hold. And they'd learn how to get the other person to face facts objectively rather than wishfully, how to maintain credibility and rapport, and how to get a commitment. Wouldn't this be valuable?

Prospect: Yes, it sounds good. I guess we all have communication problems. How long does this workshop take?

The specific question requires a specific answer. (In the previous sequence, the salesman was able to feed in progressively because the prospect regularly asked a question, agreed with, or approved of what the salesman said.)

Salesman: Three days, with a group of ten to fifteen people. Three days gives them enough guided practice in the techniques to enable them to start breaking old habits and to start acquiring the techniques as new habits on their own. Can you see where three days would be needed to start forming new habits of communicating in place of old ones?

The salesman answered directly, elaborated, and asked a question to get a reaction.

Prospect: Yes, I can see where it would take three days, and maybe more, to change old habits, but I can't take my people off the job for three days. They've got too much to do. We'd fall behind.

The prospect's objection is a cue for the salesman to draw out. Since the prospect has already given his reasons (there is too much work to be done and his people would fall behind), the salesman doesn't need to draw these out. So he uses a hypothetical ("what if") question to introduce a new premise into the prospect's thinking.

Salesman:	I can certainly understand your reluctance when there is so much to do. But what if your productivity increased by only two percent? As a result, you would get those three days back in eight months, and after that you would gain an additional three days per man every eight months.
Prospect:	How do you figure we'd gain an extra three days per man every eight months?

The salesman's draw-out remark moved the prospect to want to know more.

Salesman:	If a man were two percent more productive, he would do three days more work every eight months because three days is two percent of the 150 working days in eight months. And if productivity increased by ten percent, you'd get your investment of time back in less than two months. Do you see how you would gain three days per man every eight months if productivity increased by only two percent?

The salesman answered directly, then elaborated, then followed with a question to get a reaction.

Prospect:	Yes, I do, and it sounds good. Have you gotten this much of a productivity increase in other companies?

The prospect has asked a question, which is a cue for the salesman to feed in.

Salesman:	I don't know. It would be difficult to pin down exactly where any productivity increase came from. However, companies that have tried the workshop have asked for it again and again, indicating that they felt it was worthwhile. Many sound investment decisions are made on the basis of a little evidence and a judgment of what seems reasonable. This happens in advertising, in the education of your people, and in assigning people to particular jobs and projects. Don't

you have to make many decisions on the basis of favorable indications and reasonable judgment without having completely solid evidence for your decision?

The salesman answered the question directly, elaborated, and asked a question to get feedback.

Prospect: Yes, I suppose I have to make decisions that way fairly often. But when I take ten to fifteen people off the job for three days, I'm sticking my neck out pretty far.

The prospect's objection is a cue for the salesman to draw out the thinking behind the objection.

Salesman: I can appreciate your uneasiness since you have had no experience with this particular workshop. But how would you be risking so much when getting people to think harder, to plan more creatively, to think together point by point, to motivate each other more, and to listen to each other would increase productivity?

The salesman drew out, using the equivalent of a "why" question, after he acknowledged the prospect's uneasiness. His reason for the question pointed out the benefits of the workshop training.

Prospect: Well, what really bothers me is that these people will spend three days learning a lot of techniques, and then they won't use them.

The prospect is still objecting, so the salesman has to continue drawing out the reasoning behind the objection.

Salesman: There's always that possibility whenever people are exposed to something new. But why do you think they wouldn't continue to use the techniques when those

Case 3: Salesman Persuading Prospect 129

techniques will make more sense to them than what they've been doing all along? They'll realize that they could be communicating much more persuasively.

The salesman started by acknowledging, then drew out the prospect's premises with a "why" question, and gave the reason for his question when he referred to the people's seeing the advantage for themselves.

Prospect: That would help, but you know how some people are. They close their minds to anything new. They can't even realize the advantages to themselves of what they're supposed to be learning.

Again, the prospect has objected, and the salesman has to continue to draw out.

Salesman: It's true that some people will learn more and make better use of the techniques than others will. But if some learn all of the techniques, and some learn half of them, and others learn only to listen more and to come right to the point, wouldn't it still be worth it since it takes only a little increase in productivity to pay for the workshop many times over?

The salesman started by acknowledging, then drew out with a "what if" question, and concluded with his reason for the question.

Prospect: Yes, that's true. Even if they only use some of it afterwards, it would be a big help. I saw your fees in your literature, and they were reasonable enough. It was taking three days off the job that bothered me most.

Now that the prospect seems to be in agreement with the salesman's original proposal, the salesman should ask for a commitment.

Salesman:	What about trying the workshop with one group? I'm sure that once you try it you'll want to spread it throughout your organization.
Prospect:	Okay, we'll give it a try. I'll have to see what people I can spare for the workshop and then decide when we ought to do it.
Salesman:	Fine. When should I call you to arrange the dates?
Prospect:	Call me in about a week. I should have the information by then.
Salesman:	Thank you very much. I enjoyed our talk.

14 Case 4: Parent
Persuading Child

A. *Father Persuading Son*

A father wants his sixteen-year-old son to talk more with adults. He has noticed that Bob seldom initiates conversation with adults and that when adults address him he responds minimally. On the other hand, Bob does interact freely with his peers.

Father: Bob, why are you so quiet with grownups? You hardly say anything at all and you scarcely answer their questions.

The father has made the mistake of starting with a question. By starting with a demand for rather than with a giving of information, he hurts rapport and fails to motivate his son to pursue the conversation. The son has suddenly been asked to look within himself to examine his own motivations, and this can be uncomfortable. People need to be eased into doing this. The father begins again.

Father: There is enjoyment to be had in talking to people of all ages and backgrounds. I find I can learn a lot no matter whom I talk to, whether it's a child, an old person, or someone my age. Don't you find that to be true?

The father is leading up to his point instead of starting with it. In trying to achieve closure, to see the total picture, the son might conclude mistakenly that the father is talking about himself and is going to relate an interesting experience. Or the son might surmise that the father is merely advising him to listen to other people because he might learn something. If the son concludes that this is the whole point, he might decide there's no reason to listen further, and tune out. There is a better way to begin.

Father: Bob, if you were to talk a little more with adults when they come to the house, exchange ideas with them, ask them about themselves, and tell them about yourself, you'd find it quite enjoyable, and you'd learn some interesting things. Also, you wouldn't be giving them the impression that you're unfriendly or that you dislike them. What would you think of talking more with adults in order to gain interesting ideas and have more fun than you thought you could have, as well as showing them that you're friendly toward them?

The father started with the suggested action, then gave three end benefits, and ended with a question that repeated the suggested action and end benefits. No immediate benefit was necessary since it is obvious how the end benefits result from the suggested action.

Son: I talk to them, Dad. I just don't have much to say.

The son is objecting. The father has to resist the impulse to tell him that he hardly talks at all and that he has plenty to say. Instead the father must uncover the son's underlying thinking, both to learn what it is and to get the son to face it.

Father: You do talk to them a little. But why do you feel you don't have much to say when you could be telling them about yourself and asking them about the things they're doing?

After acknowledging something true in the son's remark, the father draws out with a "why" question and gives his opposing premises as the reason for his question.

Son: They're not going to be interested in my school life or in my social activities, and I don't know enough about their world to talk intelligently about it. We live in different worlds.

The son's objection is a cue for the father to continue to draw out.

Father: Certainly, their everyday life is different from yours in many ways. But why do you think that this difference would make them not want to talk to you? Most of them are concerned about your world because they have children about your age. Maybe they'd like to tell you about their world if you showed some interest.

The father acknowledged something true in the son's remark, followed with a "why" question, then gave his reason for the question.

Son: What do we have in common? It's hard to work up interest in other people when we don't have things in common.

The question should take priority over the objection, and the father should feed in.

Father: A number of things. You both went to school. You both have similar human needs that you want to fulfill. You both enjoy learning new things and interacting with others. Aren't these enough things in common to form a basis for your talking with each other?

The father answered the son's question directly, then elaborated, and then asked a question to get a reaction.

Son: Hell, we all have those things in common but everyone doesn't talk to everyone else. We'd bore the hell out of each other and I don't want to bore or be bored.

The father sympathizes with the son's feeling:

Father: I realize it's unpleasant to be bored or to bore others, and I appreciate your concern.

Son: I'm not saying it has to be boring but, you know, we don't all have that much in common, and conversation doesn't always come that easily.

The son's feeling has diminished. The father goes back to reasoning, drawing out the son's objection.

Father: That's true, conversation doesn't come easily with everyone, but why does that mean it shouldn't be tried? If it doesn't work, you can stop and have lost very little. And when it does work, it could be fun and quite interesting.

In his drawing out of the son's objection, the father first acknowledged something true, then asked a "why" question, and then gave the reasoning behind his question.

Son: I suppose in some cases people would find each other interesting if they tried. But we all go where we feel the chances are greatest and that we're going to get something out of it. I don't want to spend a lot of time making conversation when the chances are against me.

The father has to draw out again because the son is still objecting.

Father: I can understand your not wanting to spend a lot of time in a conversation when you feel the odds are against your making something of it. But what if it were only a matter of spending a few minutes? I'm talking about just being reasonably sociable. In some cases you might even find it interesting enough to want to pursue it further.

The father first acknowledged something plausible in the son's remark, then raised a hypothetical ("what if") question in which he introduced a new premise. Then the father gave the reason for his question.

Son: Okay, I guess I can spare a few minutes to be sociable. As you say, it might even turn out to be fun. But what do I say to your friends?

The son's agreement and his question are both cues for the father to feed in.

Father: You can answer their questions and you can ask your own. For example, since you've always had some interest in law, you can ask Tom Phillips about the kind of work he does as a lawyer. And when one of my friends asks you how things are going, instead of just saying "Okay," tell him about your last match on the debating team, what you debated about, and how you did. Or talk about your tennis game, or about the current hot topic at school. Doesn't it seem much more sociable and interesting and even easy to do, to ask one of my friends about his work, or to tell him about what you're doing?

The father answered the son's question directly, elaborated with examples, and asked a question to get a reaction.

Son: Yes, I could do that. It would be more interesting. It might even be fun. I'll give it a try.

B. Mother Persuading Daughter

A mother wants her sixteen-year-old daughter to allow more time for doing her homework. The daughter stays up late and still doesn't finish her assignments; she has become anxious and irritable, performs below her capability, and receives poorer grades than she should.

Mother: I don't want you to wait until the last minute to do your homework anymore. You don't do a good job and you get a poor grade for it. And besides you make everyone nervous. The trouble is you're doing too many other unimportant things when you should be concentrating on your studies.

Part of this opening is good. The mother did state her suggested action immediately (the daughter should leave more time for homework) and she also implied the benefits (not getting poor grades, not making everyone nervous).

However, she made a mistake in saying that the daughter is doing too many other unimportant things. The daughter may not be ready to accept this criticism, nor to give up other activities. It would be better to discuss later the reasons why the daughter leaves her work until the last minute. Furthermore, by assigning her own value to the importance of extracurricular activities, the mother may be alienating the daughter. An exploration of values should also come later.

The mother tries again.

Mother: How do you expect to get decent grades when you leave your work to the last minute? And if you don't get good grades, how are you going to get into a good college?

Here the mother begins with a question, which is a demand, when she should be giving—suggesting an action and indicating its benefit. Furthermore, she asks two questions in the same remark, a double demand that leaves the daughter uncertain as to which she should answer. As a result, she might not answer either one.

The mother makes another effort.

Case 4: Parent Persuading Child   137

Mother: In order to get into a good college, you must have good grades. And you don't get good grades just by wishing for them. You have to work for them, do well on your homework assignments, and get good marks on your tests. Isn't that right?

The daughter can only guess at what the mother is getting at. When the mother asks the question at the end of her remark, the daughter is likely to become wary, suspicious of being logically trapped into some conclusion.

Now the mother opens properly.

Mother: You are much more likely to get into the college you want to attend if you will only allow enough time to do your homework assigments, because then you will get better grades. What would you think about leaving more time to do your papers and reports in order to get into the college you choose?

The mother started with the end benefit and then suggested the action for attaining it. The immediate benefit, which told where the end benefit would come from, came next. The remark ended with a question that asked for a reaction and repeated the suggested action and end benefit.

Daughter: Sure I want to get good grades. I know it matters for college. But the trouble is that they give us too much work. I can't keep up with it, so I'm always rushing at the last minute to get it done.

The mother draws out the objection rather than argue.

Mother: Well, if they're giving you too much work, I can certainly understand your problem. But are they really giving you that much more work than you had last year? I ask because you did so much better in your grades last year.

The mother acknowledged something plausible, on an "if" basis, without agreeing. Then she drew out, using a "how much" question, and gave the reasoning for her question.

Daughter: It feels harder. I'm always rushed, trying to get it done. I guess the work is more complicated, and so it takes more time.

The daughter is objecting since she still blames the work. The mother has to draw out.

Mother: Since you're always rushed, I can understand how you might feel that you're getting more work this year. Do your friends also complain that they have more work this year? Maybe there's some other reason for your feeling rushed.

The mother acknowledged plausibility without agreeing, then she asked a quantifying question and gave the reason for the question.

Daughter: No, I guess they don't. They complained last year and they're complaining again this year, but it really isn't any more this year than it was last year. I hate to be rushed, and I always mean to leave enough time to start the assignment ahead of time. But every time I do, something always comes up, and I have to put off the assignment till the last minute.

The daughter is objecting. The mother has to continue to draw out.

Mother: Occasionally things do come up that upset even the best planning. Can you give me some examples? Maybe we can figure out a way to prevent this from happening.

Case 4: Parent Persuading Child 139

The mother acknowledged plausibility. Then she drew out with a question asking for specifics, which is similar to a quantifying question, and gave a reason for asking.

Daughter: Well, take that paper for Social Studies that was due last Friday. We had three weeks to work on it. Let me tell you about all the things that got in the way. First, there was an article I promised to write for the school paper, which had to be in a week ago. Then there were six rehearsals for the school play. I also had to study for two tests. You know I'm tutoring this little Japanese girl with her English, which I really enjoy, and which pays well. Then three or four nights were taken up with telephone calls from friends of mine who had to talk over some problems. And on weekends there are the usual things: football games on Saturday afternoons, a party Saturday night, a dance at school Friday night. And some nights there are TV programs I hate to miss, as well as the movies once in a while. A couple of afternoons got taken up with a new club at school. I want to have time to prepare my papers and reports, but I can't give up all my other activities just for school work. I don't want to become a grind who has no other interests but studying.

The daughter's objection has to be drawn out further. Her true premises, which should be acknowledged, are: these activities leave me with too little time and I don't want to be a grind. Her implied false premise, which should be drawn out, is: I have to give up either all of my activities or none of them.

Mother: I certainly agree with you that if you do all these activities, you won't have enough time for your studies. At the same time, I certainly don't want you to be a grind. But do you think that you would be a grind if you just cut down on some of these activities rather than cutting out all of them? It doesn't really have to be an all-or-nothing kind of thing.

The mother acknowledged both of the true premises. Then she drew out with the equivalent of a "why" question and gave the reason for the question.

Daughter: I thought of that, but I can't seem to give up any of these activities. They're all important to me.

The mother has to continue to draw out.

Mother: I can understand your feeling of wanting to keep them all. What would you think of keeping them all and just cutting down on the total amount of time you spend on them? For example, you could spend less time watching TV and talking on the phone. And you could cut out football games on weekends while you're rehearsing for the play and then go back to the football games when the play was over.

The mother first acknowledged plausibility by expressing understanding of a feeling. Then she drew out with a hypothetical question to see if a new premise would change the daughter's conclusion. The suggestions that follow "for example" are an extension of the question.

Daughter: I know what you're saying sounds sensible. But I can't cut my friends off on the phone when they need my help. And sometimes I need theirs, too. And the football games are fun—meeting friends, enjoying the excitement. And I want the other things, too.

The daughter's objection has to be drawn out further.

Mother: It would be great if you could hold on to everything. But since something's got to give, which is more important to you: holding on to all of these activities and giving up going to a good college, or giving up a part of these activities and getting the grades you need to get into that college?

Case 4: Parent Persuading Child   141

The mother acknowledged and then gave a reason for her question ("something's got to give"). She followed with a quantifying question, asking for a comparison. (The reason for the question may precede the question.)

Daughter: Going to college is very important to me, more important, I guess, than holding on to all of these activities. It's something I'm really set on. But do you really think I'd lose my chance to go if I didn't give up all these activities?

The daughter's question is a cue to feed in information.

Mother: Yes, I do. The grades you're getting this year are not good enough to get you into that school. Their standards are high. But your grades were good enough last year, so I know you can do it. Looking at the way you've been going this year, don't you agree that you really haven't been doing well enough?

The mother answered the yes-or-no question directly, elaborated, and followed with a question.

Daughter: I guess I haven't been doing so well this year. But I think that if I just worked a little more efficiently, I could keep all the activities and get good grades, too.

The daughter is again objecting. This calls for the mother to draw out the objection, resisting any impulse to argue.

Mother: If you could improve your efficiency enough, I would agree. How many more hours a week do you think you would need for your studies in order to get the kind of grades you were getting last year? Perhaps this will help us to see if increasing your efficiency is a realistic approach.

The mother acknowledged plausibility on an "if" basis, then drew out with a quantifying question and followed with the reason for her question.

Daughter: I think I could do it with five more hours a week.

The daughter is maintaining her objection. The mother has to continue to draw out.

Mother: Yes, five hours a week does seem plausible. That's about how much more time you were spending last year. Now, how do you intend to increase your efficiency in order to gain five hours? We all have certain ways of doing things, and sometimes we expect too much of ourselves. We can't always make all the changes we think we can.

The mother acknowledged, then drew out the daughter's doubtful implicit premise that she could make these changes, and then gave her reason for the question.

Daughter: Well, I could try to read faster and fix ideas in my mind better, so I wouldn't have to go over the material so many times. Also, I'd stop all daydreaming. I wouldn't let my mind wander.

The daughter is explaining her objection further, but she hasn't given it up. The mother must continue to draw out. The daughter's two questionable premises are: she is capable of making these changes, and making such changes could gain her five hours a week. The mother has to question at least one of these premises.

Mother: It would be fine if you could do it. Have you ever tried to do this in the past? The reason I ask is that it's quite difficult to make such changes and to keep it up for more than a few minutes.

The mother acknowledged, then asked her daughter, in effect, what she based her expectation on, and then gave the reason for her question.

Daughter: Yes, I know what you mean. I never was able to do it for very long. I guess I wouldn't be able to gain much time that way.

Since the daughter agreed, her remark is a cue to feed in information.

Mother: I agree that it's too difficult to do and that you wouldn't gain very much time even if you could do it a little. Therefore, you'll just have to cut down to some extent on your other activities. Doesn't cutting down a little make sense to you?

The mother started her feed-in remark with agreement, elaborated, and then asked a question to get a reaction.

Daughter: But how am I going to decide what to give up, and how much? I'd like to hold on to as much as I can, but I don't want to risk not getting the grades to get into college.

The daugher's question is a cue to feed in.

Mother: By taking the time you have left after you set aside enough time for your studies, and distributing this leftover time among whatever activities you want to hold on to. You might arrange these activities in order of your preference, and then go down the list, assigning the leftover time until it runs out. What do you think of setting aside time for your studies and then allocating the remainder among activities?

The mother started with a direct answer, then elaborated, and ended with a question.

Daughter: Yeah, that does make a lot of sense. I'm going to do it right away.

Mother: Fine. If you have any difficulty, I'll be glad to look over your plan with you.

15 Case 5: Teacher Persuading Pupil

A sixth-grade teacher wants one of his pupils to give more to his schoolwork. The boy doesn't ask questions, doesn't participate voluntarily in discussions, and doesn't think about the applications of what he is learning. The teacher opens correctly.

Teacher: Jimmy, you could get a lot more fun out of your work, learn more, and get better marks, if you would think more about how what you learn affects your everyday life. Instead of just copying what you read in books, you ought to tell how it applies to your own life. What do you think of using your imagination a little more if it means you'll enjoy your school work more, learn better, and get better grades?

The teacher started with the end benefits, followed with the suggested action, and ended with a question that repeated the suggested action and the end benefits. The immediate benefit is not needed here since the connection between the suggested action and the end benefit is obvious.

Pupil: I thought I was doing that, Mr. Harris. That's why I can't understand why you only gave me a C on my last report, the one about blood. I had a lot of information in there.

The pupil's objection has to be drawn out to discover his underlying thinking and to get him to face it.

145

Teacher: It's true that you did have a lot of information in your report. But did you do much thinking about how the subject applied to your own life? It seemed to me as though most of it was just copied out of an encyclopedia.

The teacher first acknowledged a true premise, then drew out with the equivalent of a "how much" question and gave the reason for his question.

Pupil: I thought about it while I read. I found it interesting. Maybe I did copy some of it, but the book explained it a lot better than I could have.

Since the pupil is still disagreeing, the teacher has to draw out the supporting premises.

Teacher: The encyclopedia might explain it better. But which do you think I care more about: how well it's explained, or how much you got out of it? You might have a wrong view of what I want from you.

After acknowledging something true, the teacher drew out with a quantifying question that asked for a comparison, and then he gave the reason for his question.

Pupil: I guess you do care more about how much I get out of it. But what did you want me to do? Could you give me an example?

The pupil's question is a cue for the teacher to feed in information.

Teacher: Yes, I can. When you explained how blood carries food and oxygen to the different parts of the body so that they can stay alive and do their work, you could have added your own ideas about why, if a person is bleeding badly, it's important to stop the bleeding. If your brain or your heart or any other part of your body didn't have blood coming to it, it would be in the same position as you would be if you didn't have air to breathe. Now can you see how thinking beyond the information you get from a book will help you get much more out of it?

The teacher started with a direct answer to the pupil's question, elaborated, and asked a question to get a reaction.

Pupil: Yeah, I see what you mean. That would make it more interesting. But it would take too much time.

Generally, when the other person objects on the basis of too much or too little of something, we should ask him to quantify.

Teacher: It's true that it would take some more time. How much more time do you think it would have taken you on this report? You may have had the feeling that it would take a lot more time than it really would have.

The teacher acknowledged, then drew out with a quantifying question and gave a reason for the question.

Pupil: I don't know. Maybe about an hour.

The pupil is continuing his objection, which has to be further drawn out.

Teacher: It might take an hour more. Don't you think that it would be worth spending another hour to make your report more interesting to the class and to yourself, to allow you to learn the material better, and to get a higher grade?

After acknowledging, the teacher drew out with a quantifying question that asked for a comparison. The reason for the question is obvious and doesn't have to be stated.

Pupil:　　　Yes, I guess it would. But I did some of that. Remember when I told how blood clots when you start bleeding, so you won't bleed to death. Remember I said that if you get a cut and it's not too big, you can hold your handkerchief over it until the blood clots and it stops bleeding. Or if it's a small cut you can just let it bleed until it stops by itself.

The pupil has shifted to disagreeing about whether he did what was wanted. His disagreement calls for drawing out.

Teacher:　　It's true that you did relate the facts about the clotting of blood to your everyday life. But do you feel that one instance is enough when you want to make the whole report interesting and you want to learn all the material?

The teacher first acknowledged something true, then drew out with a quantifying question, and followed with his reason for asking.

Pupil:　　　I suppose not, but I get impatient. I can only spend so much time with one report. There are other things I want to do. I want to play ball or watch TV or read a book.

The teacher can agree that the pupil gets impatient, but the premise, that he can't do it when he gets impatient, is doubtful and needs to be drawn out.

Teacher:　　I can understand your getting impatient and wanting to do other things. But why do you feel you can't do it just because you're impatient with it? We all make ourselves do things we don't want to do because we know it'll pay off in the long run.

The teacher first acknowledged a true premise, then drew out the thinking behind the questionable premise, then gave a reason for his question.

Pupil: I guess I could make myself do it, but it wouldn't be much fun.

The pupil is objecting again. His reasoning is: he could do it, but it wouldn't be much fun; and if something's not much fun, it's not worth doing; therefore, he shouldn't do it. (The second premise and the conclusion are implied.) The teacher could draw out on why everything has to be fun, or he could use the hypothetical ("what if") question to introduce a new premise. He does the latter.

Teacher: It isn't much fun when you have to force yourself to do something. But what if you could make it fun by making a game out of it? The more you illustrate your ideas with examples from your everyday life, the better the grade you'll win.

The teacher started with an acknowledgment of something he could agree with in the pupil's remark, then drew out with a "what if" question.

Pupil: That's a good idea. I'll try it on my next report.

The teacher now feeds in his approval and then uses an opening remark structure to introduce a new topic.

Teacher: Good, I'll look forward to seeing it. Now, there's another thing I wanted to talk to you about. If you were to volunteer your ideas more, instead of waiting for me to call on you, you'd enjoy the class more and get better grades. That's because you'd be thinking more about what was being said and what it means to you. What do you think about volunteering more often so that you'd enjoy the class better and get higher grades?

Switching to a new topic, the teacher starts with a suggested action, follows with the end benefits, states the immediate benefit (thinking more about what was being said) to explain how the pupil would gain the end benefits, and ends with a question to get a reaction, and to repeat the suggested action and end benefits.

Pupil: I feel that no one would be interested in what I have to say.

The teacher sympathizes with the pupil's feeling:

Teacher: It's hard to raise your hand when you feel you have nothing worth saying.

Pupil: Sometimes I think about raising my hand and saying something. But then I get the feeling that everybody already knows what I want to say anyway, so I figure there's no point in saying it.

The pupil's feeling has subsided. The teacher has to draw out the objection. There are two doubtful premises: everyone already knows what I want to say, and nobody would be interested in hearing me say it.

Teacher: Maybe some of the pupils would know already what you were going to say. But what makes you think that even those who do know about it wouldn't be interested in hearing you say it? Maybe they'd like to hear how you say what they're thinking.

The teacher acknowledged plausibility, drew out the second premise with a "why" question, and gave his reason for the question.

Pupil: The way I say it won't be interesting. It will just be the same thing they're thinking. No one would want to listen to it.

In drawing out this objection the teacher begins with the reason for the subsequent series of questions. He then gives the pupil perspective on the situation by getting him to look at his remarks from the viewpoint of another pupil.

Teacher: It might be helpful for you to look at this from another angle. Let me see if I can get you to do that by asking you some questions. Did you ever hear anyone in class say something that was the same as what you had in your mind?

Pupil: Yes, I did. Sometimes I'm thinking something, and then someone else says the very same thing I'm thinking.

Teacher: And did their remarks sound uninteresting to you just because you were thinking it, too?

Pupil: No, it sounded more interesting. It made me feel that my thinking was right because someone else was thinking the same thing.

Teacher: Then why wouldn't it make someone who was listening to you, and thinking the same thing, find what you say interesting and make him feel that he was right to think what he thought because you were thinking it, too?

Reversing roles is an excellent way of getting the other person to put some distance between himself and the situation so that he can view it more objectively, separating his feelings about himself from his view of the situation.

Pupil: I never thought of it that way. Maybe it would make him feel better like it makes me feel better. It might work that way, but I could never be sure that it would. Maybe everybody would laugh at what I was going to say because it really wasn't worth saying.

The objection has to be drawn out.

Teacher: No, most of us don't like to be laughed at. How often do you think people laugh in class at something that someone says? If it doesn't happen very often, it wouldn't be something to worry much about.

The teacher acknowledges, asks a quantifying question, and gives a reason for the question.

Pupil: Once in a while. Last week they laughed at Joey when he talked about getting electricity from the dams that beavers build.

The teacher has to continue to draw out.

Teacher: Yes, I remember. But would you have said something like that? If not, it seems to me that it might be because you can tell the difference between a silly remark and a sensible one.

After acknowledging, the teacher asked a hypothetical question and then indicated why he asked.

Pupil: No, I wouldn't have. I thought it was silly, too, and I laughed.

While the pupil's mind is starting to open, he still seems afraid of being laughed at. The teacher has to continue to draw out.

Teacher: I don't think you would have said that, either. Now, how often do you think of the same thing that someone else says? I'd like to make sure that you're giving yourself credit for having interesting ideas.

The teacher acknowledged, drew out with a quantifying question, and gave the reason for the question.

Pupil: Lots of times. Sometimes I even wished I had said it.

The pupil has come still further but has not yet indicated that he doesn't have to be afraid of being laughed at. The teacher has to continue to draw out.

Teacher: I get that feeling too, sometimes, when someone else says something I was thinking. But if you can tell when something is silly and not worth saying, you must also have a lot of ideas that the class would find interesting. Why do you hesitate to share them?

The teacher acknowledged, then gave the reason for the "why" question that followed.

Pupil: I don't know. Maybe I shouldn't. I guess I just don't seem to want to take the chance.

The pupil is beginning to question himself, but he hasn't opened up enough to receive a feed-in remark. When he says that he doesn't seem to want to take the chance, he is still resisting.

Teacher: I know the feeling of not wanting to take a chance, but when you don't say anything, aren't you taking a chance that others will think that you don't have any interesting ideas and that you don't know much? They're going to form impressions of you whether you say something or not.

Pupil: I never thought of that. I guess they might think I'm stupid if I don't say anything. But I'm still a little afraid they might laugh at me if I do say something. What do I do now?

The pupil's question is a cue to feed in.

Teacher: You should decide whether you want to say some interesting things so that everyone will know how smart you are, and class will be more fun, and you'll get better grades, and take the small chance that someone might laugh sometime; or whether you would rather keep silent and give up the fun of sharing your ideas, and get lower grades, just so there's no chance that anybody will laugh at you, even though they're likely

Case 5: Teacher Persuading Pupil   153

	to think you don't have anything interesting to say. Isn't this the choice you have to make?
Pupil:	The way you put it, the choice is pretty clear. I'm going to share my ideas from now on. I'm going to talk more.
Teacher:	Very good. I'll be listening for it. You know, one more thing occurs to me. Maybe your lack of confidence in your ideas is what stopped you from putting them into your reports. Maybe that's why all you did was copy information out of encyclopedias and other books. Can you see now that maybe your being afraid that others might laugh at you is connected with your not putting your own ideas into your reports?

Since the teacher and the pupil agreed, the teacher could feed in further information and then ask for a reaction from the pupil.

Pupil:	You mean that maybe I don't think much of my own ideas? I don't think they're good enough to talk about?

The questions are a cue to feed in.

Teacher:	Yes, that's what I mean. I'm also thinking that maybe you don't express your own ideas much at home or with your friends outside school. Do you think this is so?

The teacher feeds in his agreement, adds further information in elaboration, and ends with a question to get a reaction.

Pupil:	Yes, I suppose so. I mostly listen. Everybody says I'm very quiet.

Now that they agree, the teacher can feed in more information.

Teacher:	You know, just to convince yourself, because I'm convinced already, you ought to think about the ideas you

have when something is being discussed, and then compare your ideas with what other people are saying just to see if your ideas are as good and as interesting as theirs. Then, when you find that they are, you ought to try saying your ideas. I think you'll have a lot more fun doing that, and other people will think more of you, too. Can you see where trying out your ideas might lead you to sharing them more often and having more fun?

Pupil: Funny, I never thought of that. It sounds good, and I'm really going to try it. Maybe I won't be so quiet anymore.

Teacher: That's great. I'm really looking forward to hearing your ideas.

16 Persuasive Interaction
in Groups

In trying to persuade a group of people, just as in trying to persuade an individual, it is essential to come straight to the point in the opening. You should begin with a suggested action and an end benefit, quantified if possible, and follow with the immediate benefit. This motivates the group members to want to know more and immediately orients them to what's coming so that they don't jump to a wrong conclusion. Then, instead of asking a question to stimulate a reaction and to repeat your thinking, you should move ahead with the presentation of your ideas.

In persuading a group, we must constantly balance the gain of getting through to an individual member against the loss of time available for communicating with the rest of the group in doing so. The smaller the group, the more time we can allow for each question and objection.

When an objection is raised by a member of the group, a partial drawing out should encourage him to study his objection and resolve it by himself. A full drawing out would be unwise because the interest of the group as a whole might be lost.

When a question is raised, you should answer it directly and then elaborate, just as in a one-to-one conversation. However, you should not end your answer with a question since that would prolong discussion of the answer, risking loss of the group's interest. To stimulate thinking, address questions to the group. Depending upon the size of the group and the time available, you can either have someone in the group answer, or you can pause, and then answer the question yourself. Hearing the question, your listeners will have their thinking activated by their trying to find their own answers during the pause.

Questions are important tools for implanting information and the choice and location of questions should be part of the planning of your talk, whether the questions are intended for the audience to answer or are only rhetorical.

The balance of this chapter offers a case study of persuasive interaction in a business management group. The situation concerns an executive who presents a group of fifteen top-level managers with a plan for each manager to provide his subordinates with feedback on their performances. The study begins with one example of a wrong opening approach.

Executive: It's difficult for us to see ourselves as others see us. We all have illusions about ourselves and about our job performance. If we don't have a clear picture of how we're doing in the various aspects of our job, we can't know what measures to take to improve. Therefore, we need feedback on how we're doing from some source outside ourselves. And this feedback has to be in a useful form, something measurable, so that we can compare it with earlier and later feedback that we get in order to see if we are improving.

At this opening, different managers in the audience will jump to different conclusions about the purpose of the presentation. One might think the executive wants to say that they're not doing as well as they think they are; another might feel the executive is about to give an overall view of their performance. The executive does not intend to do either of these things. Here is a better opening.

Executive: We are planning to implement a performance feedback program in which each manager will set job objectives with each of his subordinates, and then continually provide to each subordinate feedback on how well he is accomplishing his objectives. This program should prove of great value to the company. A resulting increase of only two percent in each subordinate's productivity will more than make up for the estimated six percent of the manager's time this might take. And the subordinates are more likely to gain ten or even twenty percent in productivity, not just two percent. We expect this increase would come from better performance based on the new program of feedback.

The executive started with his suggested action, then presented the quantified end benefit, and concluded with the immediate benefit to explain where the end benefit would come from. In a one-to-one conversation, the executive would ask a question at this point, but in a presentation to a group, it is best not to ask a question. A question would produce a variety of individual reactions from group members, and if the executive pursued any one individual's reaction, he would lose the interest of the others. Instead, the executive should continue to feed in information.

As the executive introduces each new topic, he should move from the general to the particular. The general can be thought of as the point of the feed-in, and the particular as the elaboration that details, explains, or justifies.

Executive: The feedback to each subordinate would cover how well he is progressing toward job objectives that had been set with him by his manager. For example, if the subordinate has to send in monthly reports, the manager might discuss how promptly he submits the reports, how informative they are, and how easy they are to grasp. If the subordinate is a salesman, how well is he following the plans he laid out for achieving a projected ratio of calls to sales, for staying within an expense budget, and for allocating calls to get both repeat business and potential new business? If the subordinate is a maintenance foreman, is he doing as much preventive maintenance as he planned, does he meet his estimated completion times in making repairs, and is he adhering to his allowance for overtime? Each manager will work out with each of his subordinates the objectives for his job, and these objectives will be set up in measurable form so that evaluations can be quantified as much as possible.

The executive should now ask for questions and comments, the better to implant the ideas presented.

Executive: Before I continue, would anyone like to ask a question or make a point of some kind?

Manager 1:   It sounds like a good program, and maybe some of our managers will be able to handle it, but many of our managers know very little about setting objectives and appraising their subordinates—and especially about conducting interviews with subordinates for accomplishing these.

Manager 1 has raised an objection. The executive should make at least one draw-out remark in order to stimulate Manager 1 to think further about his objection.

Executive: I agree that many of our managers aren't skilled enough in giving feedback. What if we gave all managers training in setting objectives and conducting appraisal interviews? We are planning to have a workshop for managers in setting objectives with subordinates and conducting appraisal interviews. The workshop will be directed by an outside consultant who has done this successfully for other companies.

The executive first acknowledged, then asked a "what if" question to inject a new premise into the thinking of both the manager and the group, and then he gave the reason for his question. The executive did not wait for an answer to his draw-out question; he doesn't want to pursue further a point raised by a group member, unless a majority of the group shows interest. He used the question form to catch attention and test interest while imparting information.

Manager 2:   How often would the managers be giving feedback to their subordinates?

The question of Manager 2 is a cue for the executive to feed in information.

Executive: As often as would be helpful. Whenever a manager observes behavior that needs changing, the manager would talk to the subordinate about it. This might happen immediately after a particular task, or it might be after some pattern of behavior has been established. If the subordinate were doing particularly good work, the manager should find an opportunity to give him feedback on this. In addition, there would be a formal appraisal interview once a year, in which the manager would discuss with the subordinate his progress toward his job objectives during that year. This should be a summing up of all the feedback that had been given during the year.

The executive answered the manager's question directly with an overview statement. Then he elaborated. He did not end with a question (as he would have in a one-to-one conversation) because he did not want to pursue further the manager's question. Now the executive uses a rhetorical question, which he answers, to stimulate the group's thinking.

Executive: Now, why do we need an annual appraisal interview if we're going to give this feedback day by ᵛ day? (*Pause*) We need the once-a-year appraisal interview to give the subordinate an overview of how far he has come. The manager, too, will get to view the subordinate's performance in perspective, which may help some managers to see that they aren't giving enough feedback day by day. The appraisal interview can also be used for setting new objectives for the following year.

Up to this point the executive has been presenting information. While many meetings are for presenting information, others are intended for group members to decide together what should be done. This requires further application of the persuasive communication system.

This meeting now continues as a group discussion. At first the persuasive communication system is not used.

Manager 3: How can a manager evaluate a man's performance against pre-set objectives when the manager isn't sure whether the objectives are realistic? Maybe they were set too high, and the subordinate is being unfairly criticized for not doing enough. Or maybe they were set too low, and the subordinate isn't producing as much as he should.

Manager 4: The manager alone should set the objectives. If the subordinate knows that his performance will be judged by how well he attains his objectives, he will push for objectives that are too low. He's going to want to look good when it comes time to be evaluated.

Manager 5: If the manager and the subordinate don't agree on objectives, or on the subordinate's progress, then the manager will have to insist on his viewpoint, and the subordinate won't be persuaded, so things will still be just as they are now. They'll only make progress when they agree.

Manager 6: You can't quantify all objectives. How can you quantify the progress of a salesman's relationship with a customer when it might take a year to make a sale? You don't know whether it's the prospect's circumstances or the salesman's performance that

	makes or holds up the sale. And for the research worker, how do you quantify the quality of his research?
Manager 7:	The subordinate has got to participate in setting the objectives. If he doesn't participate, he won't accept them as realistic and he won't accept the manager's evaluation later.
Manager 8:	If the manager sets the objectives, it's going to cause trouble because the subordinate who disagrees will be resentful from the beginning.
Manager 9:	Look, are we worried about pleasing subordinates, or are we trying to get the job done? The managers know the overall situation better than the subordinates, so the managers should set the objectives and they should also evaluate the performance.

Each group member expresses his own reaction in turn, but there is no linking of minds. No one explores another person's ideas further. The discussion was a period of self-expression rather than a joint development of a plan of action.

A better way of conducting the discussion would begin with the executive's setting the rules and later reminding the group of them when necessary.

Executive:	I think we can find useful ideas for carrying out this feedback system if we have a general discussion of it. I'd like to set some ground rules for the discussion so that we think together. No one is to introduce a new idea until we finish with the idea being discussed. If someone asks a question, someone else must then answer that question before we continue. If someone presents a new idea, the next person to speak has to discuss that idea. If you want to speak, just raise your hand, and I'll call on you.
Manager 3:	How can a manager evaluate a subordinate's performance against pre-set objectives that may or may not be realistic? The manager and the subordinate can't be sure whether they're setting ap-

propriate objectives. If they are set too high, the subordinate will be criticized for not doing enough; if they are set too low, the subordinate may not be producing as much as he should.

Executive: Does someone have an answer to Bob's question?

Manager 10: The manager and the subordinate can evaluate performance against objectives because these aren't going to be exact quantities. They have to start somewhere, so they will approximate the objectives. When it's time to measure progress, they will approximate. When they evaluate progress toward objectives, they will come to realize whether the objectives were too high or too low, and they will revise them. In any case, setting objectives and quantifying them as much as possible, and then evaluating progress toward these objectives, will give a much clearer picture of the subordinate's performance and indicate where it can be improved.

Executive: Does anyone disagree with Harry's answer or have more to say about it? No? Then we can go on to another idea.

Manager 4: The manager himself should definitely set the objectives. If the subordinate knows that his performance is going to be judged by how well he progresses toward these objectives, he will want to set objectives that are low in order to make himself look good.

Executive: Jack has given an opinion and reasoning to back it up. If you agree with him, there's no point in saying so unless you have more information to add. If you disagree with him, you should question him about the part of his thinking you disagree with. Don't just state another opinion; tell him what you agree with, then ask about what you disagree with and tell him why you disagree. Your question should ask him for further reasoning.

Manager 7: If the subordinate doesn't participate in setting objectives, he won't accept them as realistic. Then he's going to resent being judged against them.

Executive:	Max, you're not asking Jack about his reasoning. You're stating your own. You're arguing with him. Let me hear you ask him to explain his reasoning in the light of your ideas.
Manager 7:	If the subordinate doesn't participate in setting objectives, won't he feel that they're unrealistic and that it's unfair to judge him against them?
Executive:	Max, you're not asking Jack about his reasoning. You're asking him to talk about your reasoning instead of his. Let's see how you feel about his reasoning. Do you think that people try to make themselves look good?
Manager 7:	Yes, I believe they do.
Executive:	Do you agree that the subordinate will try to set his objectives low in order to make himself look good?
Manager 7:	No, I don't. The subordinate knows he's going to have to justify the objectives wherever he sets them. Therefore, he knows that if he tries to set the objectives too low, it will look as though he's trying to get away with something. It will only make him look bad.
Executive:	Now, in the light of what you have just said, can you understand how Jack arrived at his conclusion that the subordinate would deliberately lower the objectives to make himself look good?
Manager 7:	No, I don't see where he got that at all.
Executive:	Then why don't you ask him, and at the same time tell him your thoughts? Start by telling him what part of his thinking you agree with.
Manager 7:	It's true that people want to make themselves look good. But why do you think they'd feel they're making themselves look good when they'd have to justify setting low objectives or look as though they're trying to get away with something?
Executive:	Very good. Jack, do you want to answer Max?
Manager 4:	I think he's got a good point. If the manager makes the subordinates justify the objectives they set, that would take care of it.
Manager 5:	What does the manager do if he and the subordi-

	nate disagree on where they should set a particular objective? or, if they disagree on the progress the subordinate has made toward a particular objective?
Manager 8:	If the manager thinks an objective should be set higher than the subordinate does, and the manager insists on his estimate, there's going to be a lot of resentment in the subordinate. And if the manager later evaluates the subordinate's progress toward that objective as poor, the subordinate's morale is going to go way down.
Executive:	That may be true, Steve, but Tom asked a question. Did you try to answer it?
Manager 8:	No, I was trying to make my own point.
Executive:	Does anyone want to answer Tom's question?
Manager 11:	If the manager and the subordinate disagree on how high a particular objective should be, they ought to explore each other's evidence, and each ought to give way where he feels the other has a better case. They have to work out some compromise that both can accept. If disagreement still remains, the manager should insist on his version being accepted and explain that he has to take responsibility for the performance of his department. But he should add that if he later finds he is wrong, he will be glad to revise the objective.
Executive:	I'd like to point out that the workshop that the managers will be taking will demonstrate how to work things through with subordinates and how to explore each other's thinking.
Manager 12:	The problem is that when we let subordinates participate in setting objectives and evaluating performance, there's always going to be some disagreement, and this is going to lead to some resentment on the part of the subordinates. No matter how well they work it out, the subordinate is going to feel that he's right on some points where the manager disagrees, and the subordinate is going to feel that he's being treated unfairly. When we let subordinates participate, we're just looking for

	trouble. We'd be better off letting the managers do it as they always have.
Manager 3:	There will be some disagreement and resentment no matter which way we do it. The important thing is to get the best results with the least possible dissension. And I say, when the subordinate participates in making the decision, he will be most motivated to carry it out.
Executive:	Bob, when you disagree with Sam, do you give him your argument or do you question him to learn his reasoning?
Manager 3:	Oh, that's right. I should have questioned him to make him justify his position. Let me try again. Sam, I agree that there will be some resentment if the subordinate participates. But won't there be even more resentment if he doesn't participate, since he won't have a chance to correct any errors the manager makes? People accept decisions more readily when they participate in making them.
Executive:	Sam, do you want to respond to that?
Manager 12:	It will all depend on how good the manager is at working with the subordinate. If the manager does a poor job, the subordinate may be more resentful than if the manager just set the objectives and did the evaluating by himself. Some of our managers have difficulties working things out with subordinates.
Manager 3:	Yes, the skill of the managers in working it out with subordinates is important. But what if we have this workshop to improve the managers' skills?
Manager 12:	I guess it's worth a try. But we'd better make sure that the managers know what they're doing.
Executive:	Good, that point was worked out very well. Does anybody else want to comment?
Manager 6:	What bothers me is that you can't quantify all the objectives. How can you quantify the progress of a salesman's relationship with a prospect when it might take a year to make a sale, and you don't know whether it's the prospect's circumstances or

the salesman's performance that's making or holding up the sale? And with a research worker, how do you quantify the quality of his research?

Manager 9: Will we have a form to guide us in estimating and quantifying objectives and in evaluating progress toward these objectives?

Executive: Joe, we can't take up your question yet. Jim's question is on the floor now. Does someone want to answer it?

Manager 2: You quantify as much as you can. With the salesman, you can quantify the number of calls he should make, the division of his calls between prospects for new business and customers for repeat business, and the allocation of calls according to potential. And you could quantify how often his call reports were in on time, how well he stayed within his expense budget, and many other things. Sure, this may not be perfect. It's hard to quantify how well the salesman relates to customers on a person-to-person basis, but even this could be given a rating, say from one to four. With the researcher, you could work out a plan for carrying out research projects and then see to what extent the researcher follows the plan. You might expect certain amounts of data to be collected in given amounts of time.

Executive: Does that answer your question, Jim?

Manager 6: Yes, I just wanted to explore this quantifying problem to see how it could be done. Fred explained it very well.

Manager 5: Should the manager and the subordinate work anything out before their meeting?

Manager 1: I don't think they ought to; if they do, their minds will be set in the ideas they work out and they won't be openminded when considering the other person's ideas.

Maanger 10: I can understand your wanting flexibility in their thinking. But what if each one were trained to make the other person justify the objectives he worked out beforehand, and later his performance

	evaluation? If he couldn't justify his results, wouldn't he come to realize that perhaps there was some merit to the other person's position?
Manager 1:	If they work out their positions beforehand, each will want to defend his position just because it's his and he put his own effort into it. They won't be looking at each other's positions objectively.
Manager 10:	A person will always be inclined to defend his own position. But which do you think is more important: not allowing any thinking beforehand, with the hope that this will eliminate any defensiveness that might still remain; or taking a chance on having some defensiveness, which might be there anyway, and having the advantage of each person's doing careful thinking about his objectives and his performance before coming to the meeting?
Manager 1:	I guess you're right. It would be better to give them a chance to think about it beforehand. At any rate, we can try it and see what happens.
Executive:	Well, I think we've accomplished a lot. We can work out the specifics in the workshop.

17 Interacting
More Productively

Communicating with Ourselves

We have within ourselves a partner who can ask questions of us, praise and criticize us, set standards for us, and evaluate our performance against these standards. This is a valuable natural resource of which we seldom take advantage. Consider this exchange during a job interview:

Interviewer: Would you tell me about yourself?
Applicant: Where shall I begin?

It would have been more productive if the applicant had first asked himself, "How shall I organize my answer? What information about me is relevant to my getting this job?" He would then have realized that his work history, education, and family situation were relevant and of interest to the interviewer in that order.

However, because he didn't consult himself, the applicant communicated a lack of initiative by leaving it to the interviewer to decide where the applicant should begin.

Interviewer: Tell me about your present job.
Applicant: I'm a salesman with a pharmaceutical company. I call on doctors and try to get them to prescribe our drugs.

The applicant only answered minimally. He did not stop to ask himself, "Why is he asking this question? What does he want to know about my present job? How would he use this information?" The applicant might then have given a fuller answer.

Applicant: I'm a salesman for a pharmaceutical company. I call on doctors to educate them about our drugs and to persuade them to prescribe our drugs. The company is quite large and offers a wide range of pharmaceuticals: antibiotics, tranquilizers, drugs for respiratory problems, and others. I've been with them three years, and I'm doing well.

The applicant should have raised a few more questions with himself: "What is the name of the company, and where is it located? How large is it in dollar volume, number of employees, and number of salesmen? What was my ranking in the sales force, in my district, or in comparison to what was expected?" He can give a still fuller answer.

Applicant: I'm a salesman for a pharmaceutical company, the XYZ Company of Chicago. We make a broad range of pharmaceuticals: antibiotics, tranquilizers, drugs for respiratory problems, and others. I sell all of these. I encourage doctors to prescribe these drugs for their patients. The company has four hundred salesmen. I've been there three years, and I've been able to surpass the quotas set for me by ten percent the first two years and fifteen percent last year. I want to leave my job because I want to get into heavy industry and do something more closely related to my electrical engineering background. I took the job because I've always had an interest in medicine, and because some friends who are pharmaceutical salesmen urged me to try it. Since I was doing well, I stayed there longer than I had intended.

Here the applicant asked himself all the relevant questions and then answered them for the interviewer. When the information he was giving seemed to him to raise a further question, he answered that for the interviewer.

Two friends are talking:

Sara: How was that movie last night?
Jane: It was pretty good. We enjoyed it. It wasn't the greatest, but it was worth seeing.

Jane might better have asked herself, "What should I look for in evaluating a movie?" That question would have prompted further questions: "Did the story hold my interest or did it drag? Was it believable? Was the acting exceptional? Was the photography outstanding? Was the movie funny? Was it supposed to be? Is there anything I could say about the direction?"

Here's a richer answer.

Jane: We liked the movie, and I think you ought to see it. It had some interesting ideas about the conflict between husband and wife when they want different things. It made you think, so that the movie stayed with you. Some characters were developed so that you felt you knew the people and knew why they acted the way they did. But the story did drag at times. Some of the acting was good, particularly that of the main character. The photography was really interesting, with scenes shot from unusual angles. And there was a haunting musical theme that kept running through the picture.

Similarly, when someone tells you something, to be sure that you've got the complete picture in your mind and that your interpretation is accurate, you should form a mental picture of what the other person is saying. Then imagine yourself explaining it to someone else. This procedure will guide you to the questions to ask in order to remove ambiguities.

A wife may tell her husband to grease the pan before cooking the meat when he makes his own dinner. If he imagines himself explaining this to someone else, which causes him to visualize his doing it, he will realize that he must ask what to grease the pan with (butter? margarine? cooking oil?).

This imaginary walking through is particularly helpful when adjectives are being used. The specific meaning of an adjective depends on reference points which may differ between the speaker and the listener.

If we consulted ourselves more fully, we would enjoy the greater use of our minds and be immensely more productive.

Defensiveness often obstructs our internal communication. If we allow it to block communication with ourselves when we don't want to face our deficiencies, we block our communications with others.

Consider this dialogue between husband and wife:

Wife: Jack, you don't spend enough time with the children. You don't take enough interest in what they're doing. You don't talk to them enough. You don't even talk to me very much anymore.

Husband: I do talk to you, and to the kids, too. But I can't spend all my time talking to you and the kids. I've got to make a living, and I've got to have a little time to myself for relaxation.

Wife: You answer me, but you don't really care much. If I'm tired, you tell me to go to sleep. If I'm bored, you tell me to watch TV or to read a book. If I've got too much to do, you tell me I've got to work out a better plan or get some help. And you do the same with the kids. You don't really talk to us, you don't respond to our feelings.

Husband: Sure, I care. I don't know exactly how you feel, so I try out some suggestions to see if they work. And the kids have their friends. They're not interested in me.

Wife: But you don't try to find out what I mean. Sometimes I'm not even sure myself. You don't try to work it out with us. You seem to want to get rid of the problem as fast as you can.

Husband: Look, I do my job. I provide well for you and the kids. I try to be a good friend and to give you advice if I can. I tell the kids what they should and should not do. I don't know what more you want.

The husband, who is not communicating with himself, isn't communicating with his wife either. He isn't asking himself whether he really understands what his wife means and what she wants. He seems to be trying to ward off her demands and to reject any suggestion that he is deficient.

Now the husband communicates with himself.

Wife: Jack, you don't talk enough with me and the children. You don't become involved with us. You don't seem to care enough.

The husband asks himself, "Do I know what she means?"

Husband: I wasn't aware of that. What do you mean by my not talking enough and not becoming involved? I thought I did give enough concern and attention to all of you, but I might be wrong.

Wife: Well, you never seem to plan activities for us on weekends or during vacations. I have to do all the thinking about that. It's as though you didn't care enough. And when I complain about something, you always give me a quick answer rather than try to find out exactly what I mean and just how I feel.

The husband may feel irritated by the criticism and start to defend himself. But if he were communicating with himself, he would stop to ask, "How do I feel about this?" He might then realize that he feels irritated, and that his irritation causes him to want to defend himself or to criticize his wife. He might then ask himself: "What will be accomplished by my defending myself or criticizing her? Do I fully understand what she wants and how she feels?" This might lead him to explore her feelings further instead of defending his position.

Husband: I'm glad you mentioned this about planning the week-ends and thinking more about entertainment. I didn't realize that this bothered you. I thought you liked to do it yourself. You mean you want me to make the plans?

Wife: No, not exactly. I'd just like you to talk them over with me so that we could plan together. I'd like you to show more interest and not just go along with what I suggest. Maybe you'd think of things you might do with the children, too. Maybe you don't notice it, but they're always talking to me about their problems and never to you. They seem to feel you don't listen very well.

If he were communicating with himself, the husband might ask himself, "How does she know that the children think I don't listen? If it's true, why do they think that?"

Husband: Okay, you've got a good idea about our planning the entertainment together. We'll do that. We might even set a specific time during the week to do it. Now what makes you think the children get the impression that I don't listen?

Wife: Well, you never say very much to them. When they talk to you, you respond only with something superficial or obvious. You don't encourage their conversation. You don't ask questions or explore their thoughts and feelings.

Again, the husband, if he were communicating with himself, would resist the impulse to deny. Instead he would ask himself, "Do I interact enough, ask them questions, explore their thoughts and feelings as much as I should?"

Husband: Maybe you're right. I'll have to watch that. If I'm not responding enough, I'll make a point of talking with them more. I'm glad you brought it up.

174 **Breaking Through to Each Other**

Meeting the Intent of the Question

When a person experiences a gap in his thinking, he isn't always sure what it is he wants to know. He may start questioning without forming his questions precisely, groping his way toward finding out specifically what questions he ought to ask. When someone asks, "What did you do last night?" he may really mean, "Why did you get home so late?" When a patient asks his doctor, "Will you be using an anesthetic?" the patient may really mean, "Will it hurt much?"

To answer a question completely, we must address ourselves to its intent. To grasp the intent of the other person's question, we might put ourselves in his place and ask ourselves, "Why would I want to know that? What answer would satisfy me?"

If the doctor had considered the intent of the question about an anesthetic, he would probably have guessed that the patient was concerned about pain, or perhaps that he feared anesthetics. If an anesthetic were not going to be used, rather than merely saying so, the doctor might reply, "No, we won't be using an anesthetic because this operation won't hurt at all. I know that it seems complicated, but there are hardly any nerves there that produce pain."

A maintenance man asks his foreman, "Are we going to be overhauling the big machine on Thursday?" The foreman might answer "yes" and let it go at that. But suppose the maintenance man asked because he wondered whether he should go on making small repairs between now and Thursday, when the big machine would be overhauled then anyway. If the foreman had asked, "Why do you ask?" they might have decided together that small but necessary repairs should be made to keep the machine operating and producing until Thursday.

When you ask a question, explain why you ask. The other person will then know how you're going to use the information and whether he is providing the information you require. By knowing why you're asking, he may also supply additional information that you need but haven't thought to ask for.

The question is a versatile and powerful tool. It can extract information, help the other person to release his feelings, stimulate and crystallize thinking, determine whether meaning has been transferred accurately, start an interaction, and spotlight essential problems.

Maintaining Our Reliability

Credibility is lost much more quickly than it is gained. If the information we gave were half wrong and half right, our credibility would be practically zero. To maintain our credibility, we probably have to be right ten times as often as we are wrong. And even with this ratio, the other person will remember the one time in ten that we're wrong.

Evaluate the source of your information before you communicate it. Did you directly observe what happened? Did someone tell you about it? If so, what is his reliability? If you read it, was the source authoritative? Did the information come through a chain of people in which each person might have made some change in repeating the information? Is your memory hazy about the information?

Before communicating, you may want to check out your information by consulting another source. And if you cite your source, the other person will know what confidence he can have in the information.

Can you trust your memory? If we remember part of something well, and part poorly, our drive toward closure will move us to fill in information from our imagination, or perhaps even convince us that we remember better than we do.

If we observe one man knocking down another and then running away, we might not actually recall later what the attacker was wearing, or whether he was tall or short or heavy or slight. Yet because of our drive that makes us want to see the whole pattern, we might provide those details from our imagination and really believe we observed them. This explains the frequent unreliability of witnesses that is often brought out in court trials.

People often confuse what they inferred with what actually

happened, and they report their inferences as direct observation. A supervisor observes a worker using a tool in a way that could break it; later, the supervisor notices that the tool is broken; still later, he tells someone that he saw the worker break the tool.

Examining our sources of information can also counter wishful thinking. When we're afraid to make a change, we often rationalize that the change will be unfavorable by pointing to undesirable things that could happen. In this event we should ask ourselves, "How do we know they will happen? What is the probability of their happening? Given that probability, is it worth making the change, considering the benefits that we stand to gain?"

Wishful thinking colors the interpretation of information. The drive to think well of ourselves is so powerful that we sometimes downgrade the reliability of information that discredits us. For example, we may attribute a self-serving motivation to someone who gives us unpopular information. If a person tells us we've done something poorly, we might defend ourselves by saying that he's prejudiced on that subject, or that he's just trying to make himself look good, or that he doesn't like us.

Identifying with the Other Person

In using this persuasive communication system, we are following the Golden Rule in communicating—to communicate unto others as you would have them communicate unto you. In accommodating for human needs in conversation, we encourage the other person to consider our thinking, to give us his, and to weigh both sides objectively. He will want to interact with us when we make it comfortable for him to do so.

In identifying with him, we accept and accommodate for his tuning out intermittently by repeating, but unobtrusively, so as not to bore him. We ask questions to make sure he has grasped what we have said.

Knowing that we don't like to be held in suspense, we come right to the point to spare another impatience and to prevent the misunderstanding that might occur if he jumped to a wrong conclusion.

When we ask the other person to do something, we tell him why. We know, from our own reaction, that simply telling him what we want him to do will leave him uncomfortably unsure until he knows why we want him to do it.

We are as specific as possible so that he isn't left groping uncertainly for our meaning; and we quantify everything as far as we can so that he can weigh one side against the other. This also demonstrates that we researched before talking to him and that we won't be wasting his time.

When we disagree with the other person, instead of arguing with him we work together to uncover what he really means. We acknowledge our acceptance of what is true or plausible in what he says, and we question what seems questionable to us. And we tell him why we question it. We reserve decision until we uncover his underlying thinking and give him ours, so that we can examine the same information together and reason jointly to a conclusion.

We answer questions directly, and we elaborate. We don't begin by explaining or justifying. And then, knowing that the other person's attention could have drifted, just as ours often does, we ask a question to make sure that he caught our answer. When we are feeding in information, we give an overview first and then go to the specifics, so that he can follow us easily.

When the other person is emotionally excited, we encourage him to talk out his feelings so that he can become more comfortable and can think more clearly. We resist the temptation to try to talk him out of his emotion, and we try, instead, to make him feel better by getting him to talk.

Persuasion does not mean manipulation. It means uncovering and examining together the basis for both our conclusions, accepting his if it makes more sense or, if it doesn't, getting him to understand the merits of ours. It also means being candid and considerate.

As a result, we think more deeply, more clearly and creatively, and we break through to each other.

Index

Feed-in remarks (*Continued*)
  Case 2A, 106–107, 112–113
  Case 2B, 114–115, 118
  Case 3, 122, 124–127
  Case 4A, 134–136
  Case 4B, 142–143
  Case 5, 146–147, 153–155
  and group persuasion, 158
  and midway cue, 71–72
  point of, 69
  priority of, 110
  and questions, 65–71

Golden Rule in communication, 26,
    177
Group persuasion, 156–168
  and examples of, 162–168
  openings, 157–158
  presenting information, 158–161
  rules for group discussion, 162
Guilt, 5, 74–75, 79

Hovland, Carl I., 25 *n.*
"How much" questions, 60, 62
  examples, 110, 139, 146
  See also Questions
Hypothetical questions, 41–43, 81,
    119, 159
  and draw-out remarks, 61–62, 64
  examples of: Case 1, 100–102
  Case 2B, 119
  Case 3, 123–124, 127–128, 130
  Case 4A, 136
  Case 4B, 141
  Case 5, 149, 152
  See also Questions

"Impulsive Closure as Reaction to
    Failure-Induced Threat"
    (Dittes), 19 *n.*
Inattention, 44–47, 178
  See also Listening
Information
  ambiguity and closure, 18, 23
  and credibility, 176–177
  and draw-out remarks, 57–63
  and group persuasion, 158–159
  loss of, 44–47
  and mental organization, 65–66
  misinterpretation of, 1–4
  presentation of, 22–28, 60, 65–
    73, 126
  superfluous, 8, 14, 26–28

See also Opening remarks
"Interruption of Behavior, The"
    (Mandler), 48 *n.*
Interruptions, 15, 26, 47–48

Judgment, 54, 56–57

Kamenetsky, Joseph, 25 *n.*
Kibbler, Robert J., 54 *n.*, 58 *n.*

Lanzetta, John T., 56 *n.*
Lipsher, David, 36 *n.*
Listening
  effort after meaning and, 22–25,
    178
  with empathy, 17
  when feeding information, 73
  and jumping to conclusions, 1–3
  passivity and, 11–12, 14, 32
  tuning in and out, 4–5, 55–57,
    177
Luchins, Abraham S., and Edith H.,
    52 *n.*

McCroskey, John, 36 *n.*
Mandell, Wallace, 25 *n.*
Mandler, George, 48 *n.*
Mental set, 52–53
Midway cue, 71–72
  See also Feed-in remarks
Morgan, J. J. B., 52 *n.*
Morrison, H. M., 45 *n.*
Morrissette, Julian, 57 *n.*
Morton, J. T., 52 *n.*
Murphy, Gardner, 35 *n.*

Objections
  dealing with, 49–53, 56–73
  and drawing out, 58–64
  examples of: Case 1, 91–94, 97–
    100
  Case 2A, 108–113
  Case 2B, 114, 116–119
  Case 3, 122–124, 127–130
  Case 4A, 133–135
  Case 4B, 138–143
  Case 5, 145–146, 148–153
  and feeding in, 65–73, 110, 114
  and group interaction, 156, 159
  rationality of, 54–55
  and "why" questions, 57, 116
Opening remarks, 22–26, 66
  examples of: Case 1, 89–90